The Day After Mugabe

Prospects for Change in Zimbabwe
Edited by Gugulethu Moyo and Mark Ashurst

Published with financial support from

Africa Research Institute

THE EDITORS
Gugulethu Moyo is a Zimbabwean lawyer who works on southern African issues for the International Bar Association. She previously worked in Harare as a lawyer for Associated Newspapers of Zimbabwe, publisher of *The Daily News*.

Mark Ashurst is director of the Africa Research Institute. He spent six years as the BBC's Africa business editor, and worked as a foreign correspondent in Africa for the *Financial Times*, *The Economist* and *Newsweek*.

ACKNOWLEDGEMENTS
The editors would like to record their deep appreciation to all the contributors to this book. No payment has been made for their work.

Most of the articles in this book appeared in earlier versions in the *Mail & Guardian* newspaper, South Africa, in the supplements "A New Zimbabwe: Imagining The Future". Africa Research Institute is grateful to the *Mail & Guardian* for its support in the publication of this book.

The article by Morgan Tsvangirai first appeared in the *Washington Times*.

The interview with Gideon Gono, governor of the Reserve Bank of Zimbabwe, first appeared in *New African* magazine.

STE Publishers kindly gave permission to publish extracts from *Fit to Govern: The native intelligence of Thabo Mbeki* by Ronald Suresh Roberts.

The directors and staff of the Royal African Society, Royal Commonwealth Society and the International Bar Association have given generously of their time and expertise to assist the publication of this book.

Published by Africa Research Institute, 2007.
ISBN No. 978 1 906329 00 6

The Africa Research Institute was founded in February 2007 to draw attention to ideas which have worked in Africa. For more information, please visit our website: www.africaresearchinstitute.org

Africa Research Institute
43 Old Queen Street
London
SW1H 9JA

CONTENTS

1. THE HOME FRONT

3. AN AFRICAN DILEMMA

4. ZIMBABWE AND THE WORLD

5. TRANSITION

CONTRIBUTORS AND COMMENTATORS

Baffour Ankomah is editor of *New African* magazine.

Mark Ashurst is director of the Africa Research Institute, London. He has worked in Africa as a journalist for the *Financial Times*, *Newsweek* and the BBC.

Dr Fareda Banda is reader in the laws of Africa at the School of Oriental and African Studies, University of London, and author of *Women, Law and Human Rights: An African Perspective*.

George Bizos is a human rights lawyer. He defended Nelson Mandela, Govan Mbeki and Walter Sisulu at the Rivonia Treason Trial of 1963-4 and has acted for MDC leader Morgan Tsvangirai.

Eric Bloch is an economist and serves as an independent adviser to the governor of the Reserve Bank of Zimbabwe.

Professor Stephen Chan teaches international relations at the School of Oriental and African Studies, University of London, and is author of *Robert Mugabe: A Life of Power and Violence*.

Brian Chikwava is a Zimbabwean writer and winner of the 2004 Caine Prize for African Writing.

Richard Dowden is director of the Royal African Society in London. He was formerly Africa editor of *The Economist*.

Mark Ellis is chief executive of the International Bar Association.

Nicole Fritz is executive director of the Southern African Litigation Centre in Johannesburg.

Judge Richard Goldstone was a member of the first Constitutional Court in South Africa, and was previously Chief Prosecutor for the International Tribunals for Rwanda and the former Yugoslavia.

Gideon Gono is governor of the Reserve Bank of Zimbabwe.

Charles Goredema is head of the Organised Crime and Money Laundering programme at the Institute for Security Studies in Cape Town, South Africa.

Professor A.C. Grayling teaches philosophy at Birkbeck College, University of London.

Priscilla Hayner is director of the Peace and Justice programme of the International Centre for Transitional Justice.

Geoff Hill is Africa bureau chief for the *Washington Times* and author of *What Happens After Mugabe?*

Lindsey Hilsum is Beijing correspondent for Channel 4 News.

Michael Holman was brought up in Rhodesia and now lives in London. He was Africa editor of the *Financial Times* 1984-2002.

Derek Ingram is a writer on Commonwealth affairs and vice-president of the Royal Commonwealth Society. He has covered every Commonwealth Heads of Government Meeting since 1969.

Dr Peter Kagwanja is acting executive director of the Democracy and Governance programme at the Human Science Research Council in Pretoria, and president of the Africa Policy Institute in Nairobi, Kenya.

Adam Kahane has mediated in conflicts in North and South America, Europe and Asia, and is the author of *Solving Tough Problems*.

Professor Tawana Kupe is dean of humanities at the University of the Witwatersrand in Johannesburg.

Dr Ibbo Mandaza is chairman of the Southern African Political and Economic Studies Trust in Harare and a former minister in the government in Zimbabwe.

Dr Beacon Mbiba is senior lecturer and leader in the Planning in Developing Countries and Transition Economies programme at Oxford Brookes University. In 2004-5, he served as an adviser to Tony Blair's Africa Commission.

Diana Mitchell was the Press and Publicity Executive officer for Zimbabwe's multi-racial Centre Party and its successor, the National Unifying Force, August 1968-1984. She is the author of a series of three biographies of African nationalists.

Gugulethu Moyo is a Zimbabwean lawyer who works on southern African issues for the International Bar Association.

Dr Jonathan Moyo is a former minister of information in Zimbabwe. He was dismissed from government in 2005 and is now independent MP for Tsholotsho in Matabeleland North.

Professor Sam Moyo is executive director of the Institute for Agrarian Studies in Harare.

Arthur Mutambara is leader of the breakaway faction of the Movement for Democratic Change.

Tawanda Mutasah is a Zimbabwean lawyer and executive director of the Open Society Initiative for Southern Africa.

Welshman Ncube is a lawyer and secretary-general of the Mutambara faction of the Movement for Democratic Change.

Nothando Ndebele is a Zimbabwean economist and executive director of Renaissance Specialist Fund Managers in Cape Town.

Professor Muna Ndulo teaches law at Cornell University Law School, New York. He has acted as a political and legal adviser to UN missions in South Africa and East Timor, and as special representative of the secretary-general in South Africa.

Joram Nyathi is deputy editor of the *Zimbabwe Independent*.

Aoiffe O'Brien is a researcher at the Africa Research Institute.

Brian Raftopoulos is former professor of development studies at the University of Zimbabwe. He is director of research and advocacy for the Solidarity Peace Trust, a Zimbabwean non-governmental organisation, based in Cape Town.

Sir Shridath 'Sonny' Ramphal was secretary-general of the Commonwealth from 1975 to 1990.

Ronald Suresh Roberts is author of *Fit to Govern: the Native Intelligence of Thabo Mbeki*.

Professor Robert Rotberg is director of the programme on intrastate conflict and conflict resolution in the Kennedy School of Government, Harvard University, and president of the World Peace Foundation. He is author of *When States Fail: Causes and Consequences*.

Dr Martin Rupiya is director of the Institute for Security Studies in Pretoria, South Africa. He previously served as a lieutenant colonel in the Zimbabwe National Defence Force.

Bill Saidi is deputy editor of *The Standard* newspaper in Zimbabwe and has been a journalist for 50 years.

Morgan Tsvangirai is president of the Movement for Democratic Change.

Hennie van Vuuren is head of the Corruption & Governance programme at the Institute for Security Studies in Cape Town, South Africa.

Phillan Zamchiya was formerly president of the Zimbabwean National Union of Students and is currently a graduate student in the land and agrarian studies department of the University of the Western Cape.

FOREWORDS

1. Long live our freedom!

Robert Gabriel Mugabe
Prime Minister-elect of the Republic of Zimbabwe
Address to the Nation on Independence Eve,
April 17th 1980

2. On tyranny

Anthony Grayling
Professor of Philosophy at Birkbeck College,
University of London
An essay on the mysteries of tyranny

Long live our freedom!

In 1980, Zimbabweans were celebrating independence and the prospect of majority rule. Prime Minister-elect **Robert Gabriel Mugabe** *anticipated the grave responsibilities of his new role in a stirring address to the nation on the eve of Independence, April 17th 1980.*

The final countdown before the launching of the new State of Zimbabwe has now begun. Only a few hours from now Zimbabwe will have become a free, independent and sovereign state, free to choose its own flight path and chart its own course to its chosen destiny.

Its people have made a democratic choice of those who, as their legitimate Government, they wish to govern them and take policy decisions as to their future. This, indeed, is the meaning of the mandate my party secured through a free and fair election, conducted in the full glare of the world's spotlight.

While my Government welcomes the mandate it has been freely given and is determined to honour it to the letter, it also accepts that the fulfillment of the tasks imposed by the mandate are only possible with the confidence, goodwill and co-operation of all of you, reinforced by the forthcoming support and encouragement of all our friends, allies and well wishers in the international community.

The march to our national independence has been a long, arduous and hazardous one. On this march countless lives have been lost and many sacrifices made. Death and suffering have been the price we have been called upon to pay for the final priceless reward of freedom and national independence. May I thank all of you who have had to suffer and sacrifice for the reward we are now getting.

Tomorrow we shall be celebrating the historic event, which our people have striven for nearly a century to achieve. Our people, young and old, men and women, black and white, living and dead, are, on this occasion, being brought together in a new form of national unity that makes them all Zimbabweans.

Independence will bestow on us a new personality, a new sovereignty, a new future and perspective, and indeed a new history and a new past. Tomorrow we are being born again: born again not as individuals but collectively as a people, nay, as a viable nation of Zimbabweans. Tomorrow is thus our birthday, the birth of a great Zimbabwe and the birth of its nation.

Tomorrow we shall cease to be men and women of the past and become men and women of the future. It's tomorrow then, not yesterday, which bears our destiny.

As we become a new people we are called to be constructive, progressive and forever forward looking, for we cannot afford to be men of yesterday, backward-looking, retrogressive and destructive. Our new nation requires of every one of us to be a new man, with a new mind, a new heart and a new spirit.

Our new mind must have a new vision and our new hearts a new love that spurns hate, and a new spirit that must unite and not divide. This to me is the human essence that must form the core of our political change and national independence.

Henceforth, you and I must strive to adapt ourselves, intellectually and spiritually, to the reality of our political change and relate to each other as brothers bound one to another by a bond of national comradeship.

If yesterday I fought as an enemy, today you have become a friend and ally with the same national interest, loyalty, rights and duties as myself. If yesterday you hated me, today you cannot avoid the love that binds you to me and me to you.

Is it not folly, therefore, that in these circumstances anybody should seek to revive the wounds and grievances of the past? The wrongs of the past must now stand forgiven and forgotten.

If ever we look to the past, let us do so for the lesson the past has taught us, namely that oppression and racism are inequities that must never again find scope in our political and social system. It could never be a correct justification that because whites oppressed us yesterday when they had power, the blacks must oppress them today because they have power. An evil remains an evil whether practised by white against black or by black against white.

Our majority rule could easily turn into inhuman rule if we oppressed, persecuted or harassed those who do not look or think like the majority of us. Democracy is never mob-rule. It is and should remain disciplined rule requiring compliance with the law and social rules. Our independence must thus not be construed as an instrument vesting individuals or groups with the right to harass and intimidate others into acting against their will.

It is not the right to negate the freedom of others to think and act as they desire. I, therefore, wish to appeal to all of you to respect each other and act in promotion of national unity rather than negation of that unity.

On Independence Day our integrated security forces will, in spite of their having only recently fought each other, be marching in step together to herald the new era of national unity and togetherness. Let this be an example for us all to follow. Indeed, let this enjoin the whole of our nation to march in perfect unison from year to year and decade to decade towards its destiny.

…May I assure you that my Government is determined to bring about meaningful change to the lives of the majority of the people in the country. But I must ask you to be patient and allow my Government time to organize programmes that will effectively yield that change.

…I now wish to pay tribute to Lord Soames, our Governor, for the most important role he has played in successfully guiding this country to elections and independence. He was, from the very onset, given a difficult and most unenviable task. And yet he performed it with remarkable ability and overwhelming dignity. I must admit that I was one of those who originally never trusted him, and yet I have now ended up not only implicitly trusting, but fondly loving him as well…

Sons and daughters of Zimbabwe, I urge you to participate fully and jubilantly in our Independence celebrations and to ensure that all our visitors are well entertained and treated with utmost hospitality. I shall be one in spirit and love, in loyalty and commitment with you all.

Forward with the Year of the People's Power!
Long live our Freedom!
Long live our Sovereignty!
Long live our Independence!

On tyranny

The old caricature of hero-turned-villain has become a familiar figure in history. Tyranny is the same everywhere, writes **A.C. Grayling,** *professor of philosophy at Birkbeck College, University of London.*

One of the mysteries of tyranny is that tyrants seem either not to realise, or not to care, that history will despise them and will make heroes of their opponents.

In today's Zimbabwe, suffering mightily under brutality and incompetence, there is just such a tyrant: the succubus figure of Robert Mugabe, changed from a saviour and liberator of his people into a bully and fool. By contrast, the police beating lately given to opposition leader Morgan Tsvangirai has elevated his status even further in the eyes of the world.

There are two standard definitions of the word "tyrant". One tells us that a tyrant is an absolute ruler, that is, one who rules without restraint or limitation. The second tells us that a tyrant is one who rules oppressively and cruelly. The nineteenth century historian of liberty, Lord Acton, famously remarked that all power corrupts, but absolute power corrupts absolutely, and history bears him out.

"Oh that the Roman people had only one neck!" complained Caligula, a sentiment that all his tribe, from Nero to Hitler, Stalin and Pol Pot, would recognise and – thinking of their enemies – applaud. No doubt Mr Mugabe thinks the same about his opponents.

The downfall of tyrannies and tyrants prompts such rejoicing that another mystery attends them, the mystery of how they ever come to exist. If people are so keen on liberty and so hate its enemies, how is it that most forms of rule throughout history have been tyrannies or the next best thing?

At least some part of the answer lies in a telling comment made by Steve Biko, six years before his death in a Pretoria police cell: "The most potent weapon in the hands of the oppressor," he said, "is the mind of the oppressed."

Once in the thrall of oppression, individuals ineluctably become its agents: they censor and police themselves; their fear makes them betrayers of others; they see their only self-defence in surrender; they carry out tyranny's murderous dictates in order to protect themselves and their families.

It takes superlative courage to resist the impulse each individual has to survive and to escape harm. The resisters of tyranny are mankind's greatest heroes.

All this goes some way towards explaining the continuing presence of tyranny. Its beginning is an even sadder matter, for it is in the laziness and inattention of majorities that tyranny finds its toehold, so that by the time people bethink themselves, it is too late to bestir themselves.

Maybe they even welcome tyranny at first. How many people believe that the answer to problems of a social, political and economic kind is a "strong leader", a guide – a Fuhrer? They only fully realise their error when the Fuhrer's leather-coated police knock on their door in the early hours.

From the tyrant's point of view, once he (or she: remember Ci Xi of China, and she was not alone) has begun on a course of oppression – of "disappearing" opponents, filling mass graves, torturing and raping, starting wars and so, inevitably and increasingly, forth – it is impossible to stop.

He rides a tiger and dare not dismount. A tragic inevitability enters the picture: the only plausible limit to a tyrant's career is death, often enough precipitated by revolution, as in Ceaucescu's case, or assassination, as in the case of Caligula and Nero. Whoever heard of a tyrant voluntarily laying down his power, unless it be to a chosen successor, an heir, intended to have as absolute a sway?

By the same token, whoever heard of a tyrant promoting gentle laws, liberties, welfare, love, enlightenment? Most tyrants know enough to provide bread and circuses to keep the mob distracted, if not content; or to keep them hard at it, at war perhaps or anyway hating others – foreigners – for the problems at home, stirring a sense of siege. Mostly, though, fear is the instrument of control, and for that a theatre of fear is essential.

A lesson taught by the events of the heady epoch of 1989 is that tyrants are merely cardboard figures when stripped of the guns and secret policemen who convey the brute impression of their power. Although everyone knows there are not enough soldiers and policemen in any tyranny to kill all the citizens if they rose as one, such things infrequently happen.

But they did, in 1989, when the figures of supposed power in one after another East European country showed themselves to be thin, impotent weaklings behind the mock-up of uniforms, medals, and dark glasses, high up on their balconies. Alas, the one place where the citizen protest did not prevail was where the movements of 1989 began: in Tiananmen Square, at the gates of the Forbidden City.

As the latest tyrant to join these infamous ranks, Robert Mugabe also invokes the earliest of tyranny's excuses for what tyranny does: namely, necessity. "Necessity, the tyrant's plea, excused his devilish deeds," suggests the English poet, John Milton. In one way this is right: staying on the tiger's back makes for many hard necessities – but these are borne by others, not the tyrant himself. That is why, when he falls, the only mourners are those who stood to gain by being his henchmen.

INTRODUCTION

Introduction

The crisis in Zimbabwe has exposed the limits of commitments to democracy and good governance at the heart of Africa's new institutions, but principle is not always at odds with pragmatism. Contributors to this book highlight the obstacles to progress and the priorities for change, write **Mark Ashurst** *and* **Gugulethu Moyo**.

Robert Gabriel Mugabe has sought to fashion a people in his own image. Most Zimbabweans are determined, principled and often socially conservative – attributes shared by the former schoolmaster who became their leader. For two decades they voted overwhelmingly for Mugabe. But in the classroom of their young nation, Zimbabwe's founding father is losing his grip.

For a man who embodied the relentless striving of the post-independence era, the twilight of Mugabe's presidency coincides with a more intractable crisis. His severity and unflinching resolve are hallmarks of a man who notched up six university degrees, yet Zimbabwe today is beset by economic collapse and bereft of self-confidence.

Like many liberation struggles, the lexicon of Zimbabwean politics is deeply religious. The redemptive promise of an equitable settlement with colonial power has been superseded by a sense of betrayal. This is a crisis of faith: a reckoning larger than any individual, but intensified in Zimbabwe by a more personal quarrel. Mugabe, who invited whites to the cabinet table at independence, feels deeply betrayed by commercial farmers who defected to Zimbabwe's emerging opposition in the late 1990s. Educated by Jesuits, the president remains a regular congregant at Catholic mass in Harare – even while religious leaders, at home and abroad, denounce him.

A more discerning separation between policy and personality might reveal new ways to navigate the political deadlock. But to date, every attempt by mediators to concentrate minds on practical questions of policy has encountered staunch antagonism from Mugabe. Discipline – always a priority for Zimbabwe's leader – has been enforced, sporadically, by violence of surgical precision. In March 2007, these assaults yet again became starkly public when opposition leaders were beaten in police custody.

Much of the emerging resistance to Mugabe's regime is located beyond the president's reach. A third of the population has emigrated, and many of the professionals and technocrats who might lead an economic recovery now swell the ranks of a growing diaspora. Whether Zimbabwe can again offer the economic and other prospects to win back this homesick diaspora will be a crucial factor in determining its future.

The economy they have left behind is in disarray. Most Zimbabweans eke out a living at the margins of the formal sector, their efforts ravaged by hyperinflation. A large proportion of the rural population survive on what they can grow from the soil, partially insulated from spiralling prices but perpetually hungry. The World Food Programme, which has been feeding Zimbabweans since 2002, estimates that four million people will need food aid by 2008. Even those in work rely increasingly on remittances of foreign currency from family and friends abroad.

The shifting loyalty of Mugabe's model pupils will not be reversed. A nation which boasted just two black engineers in 1980 has nurtured an educated middle class which, as a proportion of the population, is the biggest in Africa. Their allegiance to ZANU-PF became – in the words of one sympathetic insider – a "totalising presence" among the intellectual circles of the party hierarchy and the rural poor alike. Today, that presence has evaporated. Zimbabwe's ruling elite will remain a feature of the political landscape after Mugabe, but its near-monopoly of ideas and aspiration is irretrievably gone.

The aim of this book

This book is not a partisan project. The contributors write from diverse perspectives and none received payment. Almost all are united by criticism of Mugabe, but this is not a counsel of despair. The aim of this collection is to assess the prospects for lasting change, and to identify the policy priorities on which such change might be founded. Much of this book is devoted to analysis of what has gone wrong, for the simple reason that any useful prognosis must take account of what has gone before. As Mugabe himself stated in his eve of independence address in 1980, progress means coming to terms with history: "Independence will bestow on us a new personality, a new sovereignty, a new future and perspective, and indeed a new history and a new past."

Many attempts have been made to dislodge the elected autocracy which Mugabe has made his own. As Ibbo Mandaza chronicles in these pages, plotters within ZANU-PF have tried to unseat their president since at least the 1980s. Probably the greatest irony of Zimbabwean politics is that Mugabe has long been sustained by the support of party loyalists who, given a choice, would prefer to see him retreat into quiet retirement – if not a state funeral. Rivals with close ties to the military and state security services are known to be contemplating a challenge – although Mugabe has outmanoeuvred them before.

An alliance of vice-president Joice Mujuru, wife of the former army commander Solomon Mujuru, and her chief rival, the veteran securocrat Emmerson Mnangagwa, would pose a formidable threat. Some analysts now see a handover from Mugabe to an alliance of these contenders as the best hope of assuring an orderly transition. The view that only "insiders" can navigate a peaceful succession within Zimbabwe's military regime has some influential adherents. But as Martin Rupiya argues here, the influence and patronage of Zimbabwe's military are symptoms of the crisis, rather than its cause. Decent soldiers have been dismayed by the co-option of the military for partisan purposes, spawning a new class of thugs and profiteers. Even in the top ranks, the generals play second fiddle to the politicians within the Joint Operational Command.

Numerous other strategies have been touted to secure a "dignified" exit for Mugabe: from voluntary retirement after another election victory, to a more ceremonial role in which Mugabe steps back from the executive functions of government. The real prize in every case is the same: an exit which allows Mugabe the legacy he craves as the man who gave Zimbabweans back their land, while placing day-to-day management of a recovery plan in the hands of people with the skills and credibility to see it through. These options may have been rehearsed – behind closed doors – in talks between the ruling party and the opposition. But there is no reason to expect Mugabe will respect their deliberations. Nor even that the president is much interested in attempts to reach a negotiated settlement. From his side, ZANU-PF has been represented in successive rounds of talks by low-level party officials from outside Mugabe's inner circle.

His scepticism in this regard is well-founded. Mugabe is aware that the framework of international law has evolved substantially since the leaders of apartheid South Africa brokered a truce with the incoming African National Congress government in the early 1990s. Morgan Tsvangirai, leader of Zimbabwe's main opposition party, argues, in a newspaper article reproduced here, that amnesty from prosecution for Mugabe could be a price worth paying to secure his retirement. But any guarantee of amnesty from prosecution for human rights violations will be liable to legal challenge – either at home or abroad. Justice Richard Goldstone, chief prosecutor of the International Criminal Court and formerly on the bench of South Africa's Constitutional Court, notes that on purely legal grounds the post-apartheid settlement would be unlikely today.

Mugabe, meanwhile, is losing his cultivated demeanour. The vicious beatings meted out to opposition leaders appear to have been a tactical mistake. According to Zimbabwean lawyer Tawanda Mutasah, writing here, the foreign ministry in Harare sent a long and detailed explanation to other African governments, denying that these attacks took place at all. As Brian Raftopoulos observes, the president's self-styled posture as a latter-day folk-hero has been reduced by the television pictures of his African critics battered in police custody. The rhetoric of a brave nationalist doing battle against imperial domination is harder to sustain when the faces emerging from hospital are black.

Such are the conundrums of Zimbabwe today, a burlesque outpost of dead empire where illusion vies constantly with reality. Officially, Zimbabwe is a functional democracy. Opposition MPs sit in parliament and the MDC runs local government in urban and rural centres, albeit nominally in most cases. But elected officials lack power to bring about substantive change. In this ossified regime, dissent becomes synonymous with treachery – a proposition which, inherently, leads to violence.

In reality, Mugabe sits at the helm of a finely calibrated system of executive dictatorship, where power is a shifting centre, located somewhere between the president, the army, the state security apparatus and a diffuse network of party patronage. In this violent and stubbornly undemocratic universe, Stephen Chan, a seasoned chronicler of Zimbabwe, detects a new irony in the likely influence of Pretoria. The legacy of Mugabe's long nationalist campaign will be a country more susceptible to foreign influence than before.

Election fever

President Thabo Mbeki has argued consistently that Zimbabwe's crisis must be resolved by Zimbabweans: "We would not ever support any proposition about regime change, so that is not an option for us, whatever other people might think in the rest of the world," he told the *Financial Times* in April 2007. For the South African president, in his role as mediator on behalf of the 14-member Southern African Development Community, the best prospect of a peaceful transition is to facilitate a credible presidential election in March 2008.

Mbeki maintains that substantial progress has been made in negotiations. He has a strong interest in delivering on that claim, not least because of the intense competition at home among contenders for the presidency of South Africa's ANC, to be elected at its bi-annual Congress in December 2008. South Africa has borne the brunt of a refugee crisis on its eastern border: hundreds of thousands of Zimbabwean migrants are deported every year, and millions more encounter often bitter xenophobia from South Africa's poor. Evidence of an end to the stalemate in Zimbabwe would play well for Mbeki within his own party.

Mbeki's ambitions for the region, both in the SADC and the African Union, have also been set back by Zimbabwe's collapse. Contrary to the oft-repeated claim that South Africa's president is bound by some shared nationalist heritage to his Zimbabwean counterpart – "the same political DNA," reported *Newsweek* – the historic relationship between the ANC and Mugabe has been ambiguous. Nelson Mandela has spoken, famously, of "two kinds of nationalism", implying a distinction between the differing loyalties of Africa's liberation movements. The ANC, sponsored by Moscow throughout the Cold War and formally allied to Mugabe's rivals in Rhodesia's anti-colonial struggle, fell on the opposite side of this divide from ZANU-PF, sponsored from Beijing. Mbeki, deeply versed in this political heritage, feels no personal affinity for Mugabe: and in spite of institutional ties between their countries, Mugabe has let it be known that the feeling is mutual.

It may be inevitable, then, that the SADC mediation has been a secretive affair beset by mistrust. A tangible outcome came in September 2007, with cross-party support in the Harare parliament for Constitutional Amendment 18. The revisions will allow a ZANU-PF-dominated parliament to elect a successor to Mugabe, if the president steps down before the end of his term. Opposition support for the amendment has drawn accusations of a treacherous *volte face* from civil society groups, including the reformist National Constitutional Assembly. But the unexpected consensus in parliament is the measure of a larger ambition: MDC officials have called it a "confidence-building" gesture. The most plausible interpretation is that Mbeki has secured this concession from Mugabe's enemies in return for as yet undisclosed promises on the conduct of elections in 2008.

The opposition has little option but to watch and wait. Joram Nyathi, writing in these pages, counsels a renewed effort to bring about electoral reform, coupled with a nationwide programme of voter education. But in the face of massive intimidation, the opposition parties lack ideas, policy and organisation. A well-run election under independent scrutiny would provide an incentive to bury internal squabbles, but this seems unlikely in the wake of statements from both MDCs that their differences are irreconcilable.

In the eyes of many Zimbabweans, the opposition as a whole stands for a new kind of democratic politics, in which the legitimacy of government no longer derives solely from the liberation struggle. In 2000, Welshman Ncube, a co-founder of the MDC, won his parliamentary seat of Bulawayo North East with 21,100 votes, against 2,864 for the ZANU-PF candidate. Much of that momentum has been squandered. Even if they are spared the vicious repression of previous election campaigns in 2008, prospects for both opposition factions rest more on popular resentment of the ruling party than on any inherent strength.

Mugabe, for his part, is determined to fight on. His first hurdle will be to secure the nomination of the ZANU-PF party conference in December 2007. Rivals face a difficult choice in deciding whether to stand against their leader, although the restive mood of delegates was evident in 2006, when the party rejected a proposal from Mugabe to postpone the presidential poll in favour of simultaneous presidential and parliamentary elections in 2010. The ballot in March 2008 raises the prospect of a "legitimate" exit – either by accepting defeat or, buoyed by victory and reassured by neighbouring governments, a voluntary retirement after 28 years in power. For Mugabe, stepping down before another election would not be just a political concession: it would represent total defeat. He would rather gamble on another election to legitimate his rule.

Violence, criticism by independent observers, and even defeat at the polls have not much diminished the usefulness of the electoral process to ZANU-PF. Ncube, secretary-general of the breakaway faction, argues that Zimbabwe's deeply flawed ballots have served merely to legitimise Mugabe's hold on power. Given the record of dirty tricks, veteran journalist Bill Saidi is pessimistic about the looming campaign. In an article reproduced here, Saidi recalls the bombing and banning of *The Daily News*, the feisty independent newspaper born shortly before the parliamentary elections in 2000. In early 2007, Saidi received a bullet in the post with a note warning: "Watch your step".

The question of whether it is worth contesting elections at all has divided the MDC, although the loyalty of urban voters is entrenched. In 2005, Tsvangirai proposed boycotting elections to the Senate to demand democratic reforms. A breakaway group objected that this was ceding defeat: "Even if ZANU-PF says there is an election for a toilet caretaker we will participate," Ncube declared. Since then, both factions have continued to field election candidates – serving only to divide opposition votes. The rift has been sustained instead by ethnic loyalties, on both sides, and compounded by the snobbery of Tsvangirai's rivals. Arthur Mutambara, a more recent recruit to the opposition as leader of the second faction, has described Tsvangirai as an "intellectual midget".

Against such feuding, and with the electoral machinery very much in their favour, even ZANU-PF officials anxious for a new leader are confident of winning in 2008. Jonathan Moyo, a former minister of information, ascribes the enduring support of rural constituencies for the ruling party to the influence of "political commissars". These party officials, many of them soldiers, are conduits for a system of political patronage which encroaches on every aspect of public life: Moyo calls it "a *de facto* one-party state". But his own metamorphosis, from presidential apologist-in-chief to independent agitator, illustrates the potential for fickleness of even Mugabe's closest lieutenants.

The regional perspective
The conduct of elections in March 2008 will be an acid test of regional commitment to democracy, at a time when overall levels of public confidence in Africa's elections has faltered. *Afrobarometer*, a survey of electorates in 18 African countries published in 2006, found that six out of 10 Africans believe democracy is the best form of government. But while the number of elections on the continent continues to rise, a majority of citizens appear to be losing confidence in democratic processes. Flawed

ballots contribute to this malaise, prompting a fall in overall satisfaction with democracy to 45%, from 58% in 2001.

Better elections are the first remedy. Muna Ndulo, head of the United Nations observer mission to South Africa in 1994, argues that undemocratic regimes rarely transform themselves. More observers are not enough: electoral reform requires a longer-term approach to rehabilitating institutions of state. It is reasonable to assume that Mbeki has given assurances on this count in negotiations with opposition parties, but such guarantees will be difficult to impose on Mugabe. His intransigence throws into sharp relief the limits of the new institutional architecture adopted by the African Union (AU). Its uniform standards on governance, democracy and human rights are at odds with provisions for national sovereignty. Under AU rules, national electoral commissions are able to decide, largely without interference, on the fairness of a poll.

For the SADC, a first priority is to stabilise Zimbabwe's economy. At their summit in Lusaka, in August 2007, regional leaders agreed to develop a recovery strategy. The promise of external aid is intended as an incentive for Harare's delinquent politicians to fall into line with the SADC development agenda. Coercion may not be an option, as Michael Holman argues here in his assessment of previous interventions in African crises. But economic ruin will have the same effect. No matter how long Mugabe clings to office, nor who eventually succeeds him, the balance of influence over policy will shift over time in a direction favoured by South Africa.

The end of apartheid fundamentally changed the economic landscape of southern Africa, and Zimbabwe is out of step with the liberalizing agenda of most of its neighbours. An economist given free reign to start afresh would be tempted to scrap the worthless Zimbabwe dollar in favour of the South African rand. Pinning the decrepit currency to its mightier, fiscally disciplined neighbour would be a more convincing strategy than any amount of external credit loaned on the promise of compliant behaviour from Harare.

However attractive in theory, the notion of Zimbabwe becoming an economic outpost of South Africa is an inconceivable end to the first generation of nationalist rule in Harare. The white settlers who chose not to join the Union of South Africa in 1923, and later formed the Federation of Rhodesia and Nyasaland in 1953, laid the foundation of a nation state which will not easily be dismantled.

For all its fertile farmland, Zimbabwe is a small and landlocked economy that has depended for too long on a few key crops. Neighbouring states are moving towards economic integration and – ultimately – the creation of a single market for goods and services. Zimbabwe, nominally a participant but generally hostile to any dilution of national sovereignty, has been a liability to this project for the best part of a decade. The irony is that its educated people, high literacy rate and the second-best regional industrial infrastructure after South Africa are the basis for a real competitive advantage in an expanding regional market. If the economic outlook for southern Africa is brighter today than for several decades, as most analysts and industrialists claim, Zimbabwe's best bet is to join the fray.

Gideon Gono, governor of the Reserve Bank, voices the same confidence in his country's human and natural resources. As the crisis has deepened, Gono has assumed many of the responsibilities of a finance minister. His strategy of printing money to build irrigation systems defies economic sense, but Gono's emphasis on agricultural productivity is surely correct. In an interview reproduced here, the Reserve Bank governor gives short shrift to the government's "War on Prices" and calls for a new social contract between business, labour and the government. Although blaming the crisis on the IMF decision to remove balance of payments support for Zimbabwe is characteristic of the siege mentality among the ruling elite, Gono is likely to emerge as a key transitional figure in any new dispensation.

Until then, Zimbabwean companies rely on ingenious ways to survive. On closer inspection, economic turmoil has made local companies more dependent on other markets – notably South Africa. While the domestic economy shrinks, the value of imports to Zimbabwe has almost doubled to an average of US$2bn a year since 1998. Hyperinflation and the scarcity of hard currency have enabled anyone with access to real assets – from maize and fuel, to refrigerators and foreign exchange – to make small fortunes in the parallel markets. Companies are forced to devise alternative means of barter and exchange. Gideon Gono reveals that local companies have extended credit to foreign suppliers on terms which are not available at home: "It is the terms of international trade." One consequence is that Zimbabwe's exports to South Africa have actually increased in recent years, although the larger economy has benefited more – South Africa accounted for 55% of Zimbabwe's total imports in 2006, rising from 34% in 1998.

Zimbabwe in the world

Western influence has not helped Zimbabwe, and never less than when Britain turned a blind eye to the massacres in Matabeleland by Mugabe's notorious, North Korean-trained "5 Brigade" in the 1980s. But, as Richard Dowden argues, relations with the old colonial master are not beyond repair. Once South Africa has brokered a successor, the international development agencies will return, armed with fast-increasing aid budgets. Some of the white commercial farmers, descendants of the old Rhodesia, will return to new managerial roles – alongside the Chinese and Libyans who are Zimbabwe's new settler class.

The role of the international community is likely to be vexed: the double standards of western critics have compounded a sense of grievance among Africans. Pakistan has been a serial abuser of human rights, yet a staunch ally of the United States. Violence and intimidation at Zimbabwe's elections has been less pervasive than the blood-letting and thuggery evident in the 2007 presidential poll in Nigeria, yet the west African oil exporter heard no substantive reproach from governments in London or Washington. The point, of course, is not that Zimbabwe should be exempt from international human rights obligations, but that its critics should be more consistent.

Despite these hypocrisies, a new management in Harare will have little option but to mend its differences with the International Monetary Fund. External support for a reconstruction programme will become an important incentive in regional negotiations with Mugabe's successors: hard currency is vital to rescue the worthless Zimbabwean dollar, and international donors would support any regional initiative that delivered results.

Even so, Beacon Mbiba, a Zimbabwean adviser to former British Prime Minister Tony Blair's Commission for Africa, urges caution. In 2005, the commission urged a doubling of international aid to Africa. Zimbabwe may yet receive a significant share: western government aid agencies have held informal discussions about the substance of a recovery plan at meetings in London and Amsterdam, according to Britain's Foreign and Commonwealth Office. Mbiba points to the failure to effectively reform land ownership in Zimbabwe, as a warning against policies which depend on friends abroad.

The transition to a new kind of country will not be rushed. But such is the constitutional and economic bankruptcy of Mugabe's regime that sweeping change has become inevitable. Wole Soyinka, the Nigerian Nobel Laureate, has compared Zimbabwe to the slave plantations of the eighteenth century. Now as then, a condition of serfdom cannot go on for ever.[1]

Soyinka's comments followed the two hundredth anniversary of Britain's abolition of the slave trade. In a speech to the Commonwealth Society in London, Soyinka pointed to the sorry legacy of colonial settlement and the economic slavery apparent in the poorest parts of the developing world. The weary promises of "Never Again", uttered first in the wake of the holocaust, and again after the Rwandan genocide, have proved unequal to the rape and pillage in Darfur.

During questions, a Zimbabwean regretted that Soyinka had made no mention of the tyranny in Harare. Another member of the audience objected to Soyinka's pessimism and countered that Britons could feel proud of their country's part in sending Royal Navy ships to stop the transatlantic traffic in slaves – it was only fair, after all, to judge the protagonists of history against the standards of their own time.

Soyinka disagreed. He replied that it would be quite wrong to interpret the past according to the standards of any era other than the present. This was the first condition of progress. Enlightenment is a critique of the past. "And that," he added, "deals with the Mugabe question."

It is a vivid analogy, as Zimbabweans contemplate the bitter fruits of independence: Robert Mugabe, the great liberator, a captive of his own violent history. "He is still living on a slave plantation," concluded Soyinka. "All we can do is pray for him."

1. THE HOME FRONT

Will ZANU-PF survive after Mugabe?

The combination of a nationalist guerrilla movement with the mechanisms of colonial administration has been a recipe for disaster, writes **Ibbo Mandaza**. *But close ties to the military and security apparatus mean that only a reformed ZANU-PF can manage a peaceful transition to democracy.*

Zimbabwe's ruling party, ZANU-PF, has developed over a period of 44 years as part of the mainstream nationalist movement. Its antecedents were the African National Congress of Southern Rhodesia, the National Democratic Party (NDP), which succeeded it in 1959, and the Zimbabwe African People's Union (ZAPU) whose name was adopted in 1961 when the colonialists banned the NDP. ZANU was formed in 1963 as a breakaway from ZAPU.

A decade or so later, ZANU and ZAPU formed a broad-based guerrilla war coalition known as the Patriotic Front (PF), which in 1979 negotiated the terms of Zimbabwe's independence in constitutional talks at Lancaster House, London. But the two strands remained essentially separate in both leadership and operations. Their headquarters were in different countries, with PF-ZAPU based in Lusaka, Zambia, under the leadership of Joshua Nkomo, and ZANU-PF under Robert Mugabe in Maputo, Mozambique.

The Patriotic Front coalition became strained in the months following independence, after ZANU-PF won 57 of 100 parliamentary seats in the first general election of 1980. PF-ZAPU picked up only 18. The two parties were merged in 1987 under a Unity Accord, on terms which were less a reassertion of the former Patriotic Front coalition than a confirmation of the political dominance of Robert Mugabe and his ruling party. The name ZANU-PF was retained.

The foundations of hegemony

The power and influence of ZANU-PF emerged from the state which it inherited in 1980. The combination of a guerrilla army with the colonial apparatus of the former Rhodesia created a spectre whose full political and economic significance can be understood only with hindsight. The process was underwritten by Britain, the former colonial power, in the form of technical assistance to the security forces and public service.

Popular support for Mugabe, as the hero of the independence struggle, gave ZANU-PF legitimacy and political leverage. The ruling party was able to crush any threat to its new dispensation of One-Party-One-State-One-Leader. Like most nationalist movements of the era, ZANU-PF was intellectually and ideologically vacuous. The conflation of party and state became a life-line, which continues to bring significant benefits for ZANU-PF, including:

- Key leaders straddling positions in both party and state.
- Access to state resources and organisation.
- Deeply ingrained militarism, reflected in the Zimbabwe National Army (ZANLA).
- A self-legitimating and self-perpetuating political ideology.

This is the framework through which ZANU-PF has been able to maintain political hegemony, contest elections and replicate its systems of control and patronage. The role of the party in the independence struggle is linked, ideologically, to the birth of the state of Zimbabwe. But the Party itself lacks resources and structure, and remains essentially a shell, except at election times.

Since 2000, in particular, the Zimbabwean state has lost the capacity for democratic discourse. The situation is inimical to genuine multipartyism. Besieged by both internal and external opposition, the party-state is almost consumed by paranoia and a mentality of destructive self-defence.

Against this background, even at the height of the MDC's strength as a possible alternative to ZANU-PF in 2000, Morgan Tsvangirai had to concede that ZANU-PF was almost indispensable to Zimbabwean society. During an interview on national television in October 2000, I asked Tsvangirai what he would have done if the MDC had won the general election in June of the same year. Tsvangirai replied that he would have formed a coalition with ZANU-PF.

Tsvangirai explained that a coalition was necessary because of the control exercised by ZANU-PF over the army and security forces. The implication was that the MDC could not risk going it alone. Seven years later, the question must be asked whether the balance of forces has so altered as to render ZANU-PF more vulnerable.

The problem of succession

The confusion of party and state has frustrated attempts to unseat Mugabe. The difficulties of succession owe less to the idiosyncrasies of an incumbent who would like to die in office, than to the organisational weakness of ZANU-PF compared to the state. This confusion provides a loose but convenient framework through which Mugabe has been able to retain control. The Cabinet, the ZANU-PF Politburo and the party's Central Committee have become instruments through which to pre-empt or manage dissent. Patronage keeps the state apparatus well greased.

However, debate over the succession within ZANU-PF has simmered under the surface since at least 1987, when Mugabe became the executive president. Veteran nationalists Eddison Zvobgo, Emmerson Mnangagwa, Sydney Sekeramai and John Nkomo were mentioned, variously, as possible contenders in the vain expectation that Mugabe would retire by the turn of the 1990s.

Every ZANU-PF Congress since 1994 has held out the possibility of discussion, or even decision, on a plan for succession. This has never materialised, although most members of the party hierarchy have never been reconciled to the idea of a president-for-life. Many were understandably lukewarm in their response to Mugabe's presidential bid in 2002.

Eddison Zvobgo, speaking at a colleague's funeral shortly before the elections of 2002, likened the president's refusal to hand over power to "the mentality of a madman who, when given a baton in a race, flees with it into the mountains instead of passing it on." Interviewed in December 2003, Zvobgo told me that Mugabe had no concept of succession but would, if necessary, "raze the entire country to the ground in order to stay in power". Sadly, Mugabe has almost done just that.

The Tsholotsho succession bid

The issue of succession came to a head in the months leading to the ZANU-PF Congress of December 2004. Two expectations developed, unstated, within the party. First, that Mugabe would retire at the end of his term in March 2008. Second, that whoever was elected by Congress to the vacant post of party vice-president would be Mugabe's successor.

The contest for vice-president was between Emmerson Mnangagwa and Joice Mujuru. According to party insiders, by August 2004 Mnangagwa had secured support from seven of Zimbabwe's ten provinces. Joice Mujuru was a surprise candidate supported by the Women's Congress, on the strength of a resolution passed in 1999 requiring one of the two vice-presidents to be a woman.

In the face of this belated challenge, Mnangagwa's supporters, led by Jonathan Moyo and other party heavyweights, organised a meeting at Tsholotsho in western Zimbabwe. Their plan, which became known as the "Tsholotsho succession bid", was to oust vice-president Joseph Msika and national chairman John Nkomo in order to prevent the election of Joice Mujuru as second vice-president. The vice-presidential positions were to be contested by Emmerson Mnangagwa and Thenjiwe Lesabe, with Patrick Chinamasa standing for national chairman and Jonathan Moyo running for the position of secretary for administration (in effect, secretary-general).

> *"The president's refusal to hand over power has been likened to the mentality of a madman who, when given a baton in a race, flees with it into the mountains instead of passing it on."*

Mugabe found himself caught between the "Tsholotsho gang" on the one hand and, on the other, Joice and Solomon Mujuru, various political allies across the ten provinces, and their loyalists in the military and security. Most of the "Tsholotsho gang" were exposed by December 2004, and their plan did not succeed. Joseph Msika and John Nkomo retained their posts. Joice Mujuru emerged as vice president in both party and state. In his closing remarks at the Congress, Mugabe inferred that Joice Mujuru had become his successor. Amid applause, he told her to look beyond being just a vice-president.

A balance of forces

The key question raised by the 2004 Congress is to what extent did the outcome of the party elections represent a long-term victory for the ZANLA power bloc within

ZANU-PF, represented by Solomon and Joice Mujuru? Did the victory of this army faction upset whatever game-plan Mugabe himself had in mind, including the objective of extending his term of office beyond 2008?

The two-year period between Congress in 2004 and ZANU-PF's annual conference of December 2006 demonstrated that Mugabe had not yet decided to step down, either as party leader or as head of state. Joice Mujuru's prospects of moving into State House were anything but a *fait accompli*.

At the December 2006 annual Conference, in Goromonzi, party members were surprised when Mugabe tabled a motion to extend his term of office from 2008 to 2010. However, the same elements which had defeated the "Tsholotsho" agenda resisted the 2010 plan. Within the party, calls grew louder for Mugabe to quit at the end of his current term. Mugabe himself had intimated in various interviews, albeit outside the country, that he was preparing to leave office. Veteran nationalists Enos Nkala and Edgar Tekere added their weight to demands that Mugabe concede to a peaceful succession.

In a broadcast interview on February 20th 2007, Mugabe accused his detractors inside and outside the Party of unbridled ambition and impatience. He said that he was not going to be "pushed out" prematurely, and expectations that Joice Mujuru would soon succeed him were mistaken. "If I want to lengthen my term I can stand next year [2008] – what prevents me from standing and beating?" Mugabe concluded, "I can stand and then have another six years for that matter..."

Mugabe is fully aware that a significant section – perhaps even a majority – of the party leadership, senior military and the security hierarchy want him to retire at the end of his term in 2008. These are, after all, the same elements within the party which forced him to drop his bid to extend his current term of office from 2008 to 2010. Those campaigning for Mugabe's retirement argue that:

- Mugabe has overstayed his usefulness as leader of party and state.
- He lacks the skills to tackle the political and economic malaise.
- Zimbabwe's fortunes can be revived under a new chief executive.
- A change in leadership will save ZANU-PF from almost certain doom if he stays.
- His retirement would inspire the entire nation, heralding a new era in Zimbabwe.

Notwithstanding these arguments, opinion in ZANU-PF is divided ahead of the Extraordinary Congress in December 2007. A campaign to endorse Mugabe is gathering momentum, led by junior members of the Politburo. Elliot Manyika and Nicholas Goche, respectively of the Party Commissariat and Security structures, are said to have forged an alliance with Emmerson Mnangagwa and others from the "Tsholotsho gang".

Press reports have suggested that this pro-Mugabe campaign has the support of key figures in the public service. George Charamba, permanent secretary in the department of information and publicity, and a member of the "Tsholotsho gang", has promoted a pro-Mugabe campaign in the state media. These efforts coincide with speculation that the pro-Mugabe lobby favours a "Third Way", under which the president will help one of their own – possibly Emmerson Mnangagwa – to emerge as his successor. This scenario is made more likely by Constitutional Amendment 18, passed by parliament in September 2007, which allows parliament to approve a successor should Mugabe choose to retire.

Ultimately, the outcome of the December 2007 Congress will depend on Mugabe himself. He can decide to stand down before or during the Congress to allow a pro-Mugabe lobby to nominate his successor. But he is equally likely to put pressure on Congress to endorse him, knowing that most of his opponents will defer a challenge for fear of openly dividing and destroying the party. Whether or not Congress succumbs to this pressure, the attempt to secure another nomination for Mugabe would cause serious division. With or without Mugabe as candidate, such a rift would negatively affect ZANU-PF's prospects at elections in 2008 and threaten its survival thereafter.

A way forward

The existence of ZANU-PF as a party is closely tied to its control of the state. Therefore, it is doubtful the party can continue to exist in the event that it loses power. Amendment 18 of the Constitution of Zimbabwe goes a long way towards guaranteeing ZANU-PF's hold on power, even after Mugabe has gone.

The future of both Mugabe and ZANU-PF will be determined at the Extraordinary Congress to be held in December 2007. This will be a watershed in the history of ZANU-PF. Mugabe's survival as leader, and indeed all that is being done now to secure his victory at the next election, is also a contest for the preservation and survival of ZANU-PF. But all depends on whether ZANU-PF can win the crucial next election in 2008.

An orderly and peaceful succession will almost guarantee that ZANU-PF wins the elections in 2008 and thereby retains control of the state. But Zimbabwe is on the threshold of great changes. The transition from Robert Mugabe and the era of the founding nationalists to a new generation of leaders is already underway.

Zimbabwe will reach a turning point, possibly in 2008. The opportunity exists for a period of national healing during which recrimination between parties and antagonism between state and civil society will begin to recede, facilitated by a unity government.

In this scenario, ZANU-PF will work with the opposition during a transitional period leading to the next general election. A new leadership, fully aware of the political and economic problems of the past, will break away from the current trajectory. A substantive infusion of technocratic skills, particularly in the economic departments of government, will facilitate planning of a recovery programme. The return of 3.8 million Zimbabweans now in the diaspora, will bring both skills and resources to invest in the economy, firmly supported by the international community.

Dr **Ibbo Mandaza** *is chairman of the Southern African Political and Economic Studies Trust in Harare and a former minister in the government in Zimbabwe.*

The Mugabe way

Zimbabwe's political system bears the hallmarks of a one-party state. Despite pressure for fair elections, Mugabe commands every advantage at the ballot box, writes former minister of information **Jonathan Moyo**.

Every crisis has a history. In 1980, soon after replacing Ian Smith as prime minister, Mugabe embarked on the creation of a legislated one-party state. He disbanded the government of national unity. He launched *Gukurahundi*, a single-minded military campaign in the Matabeleland and Midlands provinces, stronghold of the rival PF-ZAPU party. In 1987, PF-ZAPU nationalists finally succumbed to a "merger" with ZANU-PF, under a treacherous Unity Accord. Its key tenet was to prepare for a one-party state under an executive president.

Mugabe morphed from prime minister into a lifelong head of state in the image of Kamuzu Banda, of Malawi. But his hope of creating a legislated one-party state began to recede in the 1990s, in the wake of new national, regional and international developments. In Zimbabwe, the adoption of an Economic Structural Adjustment Programme brought unpopular austerity measures. Further south, the Convention for a Democratic South Africa (CODESA) negotiations in South Africa led ineluctably to Nelson Mandela's release and election as a democratic president. After the Cold War, pro-democracy movements proliferated throughout Africa.

Nevertheless, the political and institutional foundations of a one-party state had been laid in Zimbabwe. ZANU-PF was weakened as a political party with functional structures among the grassroots, while control of state institutions was concentrated in the hands of people reporting directly to the president. This is the essence of the "Mugabe way".

The courageous nationalists with impeccable liberation credentials, who could have successfully sought the ZANU-PF leadership, are now either dead or ousted from the ruling party. But once loyal or harmless factions, such as those represented by the retired General Solomon Mujuru and Emmerson Mnangagwa, now have a clear opportunity. They are likely, if not certain, to squander that opportunity. Lacking either the stature or the policies to better Mugabe, both fear the consequences of breaking ranks. They are afraid of taking the bull by its horns, knowing they would be crushed to oblivion.

Nor can pretenders to Mugabe's throne count on a fair chance in elections. The "Mugabe way" does not necessarily mean rigging elections in the ordinary sense of the term. Instead, a raft of institutional and organisational tricks ensures opposition candidates cannot compete freely against Mugabe's direct supervision of the political machine.

Take, for example, the presidential election in 2002. The military deployed scores of personnel at every village across the country. They became, in effect, Mugabe's political commissars – the political lifeblood of the ZANU-PF campaign. They were able to command authority over village headmen, chiefs, headmasters and heads of government departments. Villagers were routinely told to declare themselves illiterate at polling stations, a signal for "assistance" from polling officers who would "know what to do".

When the votes were counted, Mugabe won the 2002 election by a paltry 400,000 votes. Given the huge margins of his previous victories, in 1990 and 1995, it is hard to conceive of this result without the assistance of ZANU-PF's military commissars. The "Mugabe way" has become deeply institutionalised.

This is the stark reality which Mbeki confronts in his role as a mediator for the SADC region. Besides the military, police and intelligence services, at least 14 government ministries do "commissariat" work to defend Mugabe. This makes it difficult to challenge him from within his own party, and harder still to mobilise popular opposition at national polls. Indeed, without these mechanisms of a *de facto* one-party state, Mugabe has no chance of winning in 2008.

Extracted from an article first published in the *Mail & Guardian*, April 13th 2007, and edited for clarity.

Back to the future

A way out of the political gridlock will not be brokered by Zimbabwe's political parties alone. The great nationalist project will have led to foreign influence of a new and greater sort than ever before, argues **Stephen Chan**.

With or without Robert Gabriel Mugabe, Zimbabwe is not at a point where it can sink no further. Zaïre under Mobutu, Uganda in the aftermath of Amin, genocide in Rwanda, and the civil wars of Liberia and Sierra Leone all stand as examples of the worse that could still come.

Powerful actors on all sides in Zimbabwe are realising that worse must not come. If their influence and interests are to survive, the future has to be rescued from the hands of the current president. The last sacrifice in the struggle for national liberation will be Mugabe himself, the father of the nationalist movement.

Within Mugabe's own party, ZANU-PF, frantic realignments took place in early to mid-2007. Among the aspiring successors, several shared a common history. Solomon Mujuru, the retired army commander, and his wife Joice Mujuru, currently vice-president, command significant military credentials. Many top soldiers are behind them.

Their hands would be stronger still if Didymus Mutasa, minister of security and architect of much of the current internal repression, chooses to throw his hat into their ring. An alliance with Mutasa would bring the Central Intelligence Organisation onto the side of the Mujurus.

The chief rival to the Mujuru camp is Emerson Mnangagwa, minister of rural housing and a former defence minister. He can draw on his own military alliances. If Mnangagwa opts to cooperate with the Mujurus, their combined resources would command decisive, coercive force in the military and security agencies.

Together, these factions would present a formidable inducement to Mugabe not to persevere beyond 2008. But their triumph would become the triumph of coercive powers. Securocrats would run Zimbabwe, and that would not be a good omen for democracy.

Mugabe had good reason to seek to divide and rule these two factions, and by mid-2007 his efforts appeared successful. Separately – as insurance against any attempt to force his hand – Mugabe had fashioned his own presidential force, known as the "Green Bombers", from ZANU-PF's youth militia. This tactic mimicked the last act of Prime Minister Abel Muzorewa, who assembled a personal militia in the final days of Ian Smith's minority white regime.

Relying on this method of brutal political policing alone would have been a sign of desperation. The "Bombers" are neither disciplined, nor heavily armed. If it had come to a fight, with Mugabe refusing to go, it would not have been civil war – the Bombers could never withstand an organised military push. But they could cause much bloodshed in a showdown.

Instead, the sheer combination of divisions between the Mujurus and Mnangagwa, and the fiercely-disciplined sense of party within ZANU-PF, meant that Mugabe could stand his ground without physical conflict. This is something under-appreciated by the West. There are some seven factions within the party, of which those with military backing are the strongest. But all the factions will refuse, beyond a certain key point, to destabilise the party.

Know thy neighbour

Party discipline, modelled on the methods of guerrilla warfare, is a phenomenon recognised by the ANC in South Africa. This is why Mbeki and his ANC colleagues spend more time talking to what they hope will become the influential factions within ZANU-PF than to the two opposition MDCs. The struggle for influence is unabating.

South Africa has also bolstered the position of Gideon Gono, governor of the Reserve Bank. He remains a contender for high political office because the South Africans want him to remain in the mix. Gono is the only fiscal discipline left, even if that is not very much. It is on people like him that the South Africans know that the recovery must be built.

When can that recovery start? Not while Mugabe is still at the helm. And Mugabe is in a belligerent mood. His fighting talk has become more militant, and the lashing out – both verbal, and in attacks on the opposition – marks a departure from his former style. Previously, Mugabe had always sought to give an impression of being in control. He acted calmly, preferring to taunt his opponents with disdainful sarcasm. There is no sarcasm now.

The opposition – the two MDCs – claim to be interested in rebuilding unity, or at least uniting behind a single presidential candidate. But neither faction sustained this impetus much beyond the united protests of early March. They have a powerful incentive to cooperate if they are to secure an effective role in the political brokering that lies ahead.

The South Africans had hoped Mugabe might stand down by August 2007, provided he received certain guarantees of immunity from prosecution in his retirement. Mugabe did not want to confront the fate of Chiluba in Zambia – who was prosecuted for fraud after leaving office – or the former Liberian president, Charles Taylor. Taylor was promised a quiet exile in Nigeria, but is now on trial at The Hague.

During negotiations in 2007, South African mediators attempted to win assurances of immunities and a safe retirement for Mugabe. They had no answer to the fears Mugabe raised based on Taylor. But even most members of the opposition would accept immunities for Mugabe. Everyone knows nothing can restart with him on the scene.

Morgan Tsvangirai has, as ever, shown immense courage; and even Arthur Mutambara has now been blooded. The larger ambition of the opposition movements was not just to bring down Mugabe, but to democratise Zimbabwean politics. But the two MDCs have been ineffectual for so long that there is no reason to predict a "last push" sufficient to topple the old president.

In the absence of an effective opposition, it will be the South Africans who will call some decisive shots. But whatever the outcome, the horse-trading that must follow Mugabe's departure will not be very democratic.

South Africa has long sought a unity government. They would be happy with a coalition involving the Mujurus, Mnangagwa and Tsvangirai. While they do not have a strong view on Mutambara, they assume that it is better to have all the "name" actors inside the government, rather than outside.

Tactics for an endgame

This emphasis on inclusivity will make it easier, in the post-Mugabe period, for South Africa to guide Zimbabwe into a new era of political transition. There is not much Zimbabweans will be able to do to resist. The great nationalist project will have led to foreign influence of a new – and greater – sort than ever before.

For the international community, this is likely to be enough. Whether one of the Mujurus, Mnangagwa, Tsvangirai or Mutambara is president is a smaller issue. The departure of Mugabe will be a symbolic moment for the West. Aid and investment will, slowly, resume. But this begs a terrible question: was the West prepared to sacrifice so many Zimbabwean lives merely because of its argument with Robert Mugabe? The answer, probably, is "Yes".

The synchronicity of Mugabe and Tony Blair both leaving office within the same contemporary epoch would be truly symbolic. The timing, however, remains far from certain. Dissidents within ZANU-PF are not yet ready to force Mugabe out. The two MDCs are not sufficiently organised. The president, meanwhile, is fiercely resisting.

An alternative strategy for Mugabe's opponents is to prevent him from his stated intention of running again as president in 2008. Even waiting until an election in March 2008 entails a high price. It might seem abstract, but there really is a big difference between inflation at – say – 5,000 or 10,000% and inflation at double that rate again.

Many in today's Zimbabwean elite will not feel like much of an elite for much longer. All the parallel-market manoeuvrings cannot be a long-term solution, even for those who have profited from the economic meltdown. Finally, there is only so much foreign exchange available to be transacted. If there is nothing left for "millionaires" to buy, of what use are the millions and prospective billions of Zimbabwean dollars?

The prospects of a so-called elegant solution are fading. There will not now be a combination of both ZANU-PF dissidents and opposition MDC leaders inviting a visiting delegation of high-level African Union presidents to "persuade" Mugabe into honourable retirement. Everyone, especially the South Africans, are counting down to the March 2008 elections.

The South African strategy implies two distinct prospects. First, with a "clean" (or cleaner) election, there remains a strong likelihood that Mugabe will win. The stubbornness of ZANU-PF party discipline, and its capacity to mobilise support, is stronger than anything the divided MDCs can muster. Second, the South Africans hope that, having won a final endorsement, Mugabe can then be persuaded to stand down with "honour". By then, they expect to have worked out the package of immunities necessary to persuade him to go.

Yet, even if this can be arranged, it is unlikely Mugabe will go with any happiness. The image of a bitter old black man as an exact parallel of that bitter old white man, Ian Smith, is a miserable record for posterity. But this is the image history is likely to retain: Mugabe, the ruthless liberation leader who, after the war was won, combined ruthlessness with, for a time, highly successful government, but who, in the end, sacrificed reality for his dream of a completed nationalism.

The president, with his defiant moustache and beautifully cut suits, has soft hands. I have noticed these hands. They are not hands that held a hoe or spade. They do not remember how. They are hands that are used to eat with good manners and daintily.

Perhaps, when he embarked upon the seizures of land in 2000, Mugabe felt the angel of death at his shoulder. He wanted to complete his life's work. Instead, his actions have overturned the economic foundations of an independent country. Whoever next holds power in Zimbabwe might still think like a Jesuit, but should plan like a farmer – and grow food for his neighbour.

Stephen Chan *is professor of international relations at the School of Oriental and African Studies, University of London, and author of* Robert Mugabe: A Life of Power and Violence *(I.B. Tauris, 2003). He was a member of the Commonwealth Observer Group to Zimbabwe in 1980.*

There's still time for Mugabe...but not much!

A promise of immunity for crimes committed during his tenure would remove one obstacle to Mugabe's departure, writes **Morgan Tsvangirai**. *The leader of the opposition Movement for Democratic Change is ready to negotiate, but not to join Mugabe's side.*

The world's outcry at the brutality exhibited by the regime of President Robert Mugabe has been heartening to the Zimbabwean people. Make no mistake, this condemnation, both in Africa and abroad, has had a huge and positive effect on the morale of those fighting for freedom.

True, there have been worse leaders in the world. According to the Guinness Book of Records, Joseph Stalin killed more than 30 million people. Idi Amin, murdered around 300,000 Ugandans, while one in ten Cambodians perished under the rule of Pol Pot. Stalin, Amin and Pol Pot lived out their lives in relative comfort and died of natural causes.

Nevertheless, the world has changed. General Augusto Pinochet of Chile, propped up so shamelessly by Washington and Europe during the Cold War, ended up on trial, stripped of the immunity he had forced the Argentine government to give him in exchange for a transfer to democracy.

On my own continent, the former leadership of Rwanda and Sierra Leone are in the dock, while one-time president of Liberia, Charles Taylor, is under arrest at the Hague for crimes against humanity. These are dangerous times for dictators.

I have little doubt that one reason Robert Mugabe is so determined to stay in office until he dies is a fear of prosecution. In the early '80s, he sent his army into our southern province of Matabeleland where it slaughtered thousands of people loyal to his rival, the late Dr Joshua Nkomo.

Mugabe was not alone. Air Marshall Perence Shiri amongst others, led the Matabele genocide; speaker of Parliament, Emmerson Mnangagwa, oversaw it as minister; various heads of the feared Central Intelligence Organisation, or CIO, including the incumbent Didymus Mutasa, were implicated.

These individuals could be held responsible for permitting acts of torture and abuse, not to mention the wholesale displacement of an estimated 1.5 million people when their homes were bulldozed in 2005 during "Operation *Murambatsvina*" (clear the trash).

And that's the Catch-22! If we say we'll bring these people to justice, they will cling ever more firmly to power. Yet, if we offer them unconditional pardon, we sell out the hopes of their victims: millions of people who have a right to justice.

I am reminded of the words of Henry Kissinger when he was secretary of state in the 1970s: "If you want to make peace, it's no good talking to your friends; you need to speak with your enemies."

To this end we are willing at any time to sit down with Mugabe and his ministers and discuss a transfer to democracy, free and fair elections, an end to their rigid control of the media and a new era of freedom for Zimbabwe. If it took immunity from prosecution to secure change, we could talk about that.

Our side comes to the table with no preconditions except that discussion must be aimed at bringing true freedom to the country. I will never be bought off by offers to join Mugabe's side, or any plan that would see a continuation of the current tyranny.

There is still time for Mr Mugabe to make a dignified exit, but not much. Beatings, torture, killings, rigged elections and control of the media may secure his position in the short term, but nothing will change the outcome.

Let's pray that Africa and the world can persuade him of that before it is too late.

Extracted from an article first published in *The Washington Times*, May 4th 2007, and edited for clarity.

Lessons in violence

Fears of a "messy" transition have bolstered Mugabe's determination to plan an exit on his own terms. Regional mediation is more coordinated, but the Movement for Democratic Change is divided and lacks direction, writes **Brian Raftopoulos**.

Among many reports of violent assaults on Zimbabwe's opposition, one remains fixed in my mind. The day after his release from police custody in March 2007, I received an SMS message from Tendai Biti, secretary-general of Morgan Tsvangirai's MDC. These are his words:

> The assault was so surreal that even at this stage I haven't yet come to terms with it. In the particular case of Morgan Tsvangirai, Grace Kwinjeh and Lovemore Madhuku the intention was to kill. In my case they hit me so much and only stopped at the insistence of other on-looking policemen. Two amazing things. None of us cried during the murder attempts. Secondly we were so helpless against the brutality no-one could defend the other. Our spirits are not broken. I know we will be back on the streets again. Maybe this time they will finish the unfinished business. Who cares?

The answer to Biti's question lies in the widespread condemnation provoked by the Mugabe regime. The hubris of these attacks signalled a new degree of intimidation, affirming Mugabe's often-quoted remark that he holds "a degree in violence". It was almost as if the uninhibited and public assault on MDC leaders was the impetus that a frustrated African and western diplomatic community had needed.

Beyond a giddy need – a euphoria – for change from within the country, there has been a convergence of national, regional and international forces to call for a new political dispensation. This is the context in which Zimbabwe is described as close to a "tipping point". Given the balance of political forces, however, it is also clear that Zimbabwe faces a very messy and difficult "transition" after Mugabe.

There is certainly more discord within the ruling party than at any stage during the post-colonial period, focused on the stubborn, but politically weakened, figure of Mugabe. When autocratic ruling parties are confronted with a growing array of opposition and resistance, party structures which once acquiesced in the centralisation of power predictably begin to rebel. We have seen a similar process in Kenya and Malawi, and in eastern Europe in Bulgaria and Romania.

The end of monopoly power

ZANU-PF has a long history of fractiousness and violent internal conflicts. The party was never a monolithic structure, and Mugabe has relied on a close relationship with the military to retain power since taking up the reins in the late 1970s. He spent the first decade of independence consolidating his position. This was achieved at the expense of developing any democratic framework in either the Zimbabwean state or within the party.

> *"The threat of internal conflicts within the military poses the greatest risk to regional security – and in particular to South Africa."*

The monopoly of leadership power now poses a threat to the survival of other interests within ZANU-PF. Mugabe has a record of dealing firmly with opposition from within his own ranks, although most of the historic challengers were weak. The biography of his erstwhile ally and party founder, Edgar Tekere, reveals as much about the poverty of alternatives to Mugabe – not least Tekere himself – as about the machinations of the president.

More recently, the balance of power has changed. Mugabe has found himself confronted by internal factions that have a base within the army and security organs. Although these lack a credible national political presence in Zimbabwe, it is probably this threat of internal conflicts within the military that poses the greatest risk to regional security – and in particular to South Africa.

In response, Mugabe has attempted to re-energise the war veterans who have spearheaded his campaign of state violence during the land seizures which began in 1999. Authoritarian reconfiguration of state power is a zero-sum game, which Mugabe has made his own. Joseph Chinotimba, leader of the war veterans, has made clear exactly how much is at stake in his counsel to fellow war veterans: "Comrades, if the President goes next year most of us will be hanged. If he goes we will go down with him. We have to campaign for him."

Against negotiation

It is unlikely that Mugabe will feel himself reaching the end of his road, and more likely that he will isolate his critics in the party. He is determined to plan an exit on terms more of his own making. One strategy is to try again to build consensus for his proposal to defer elections until 2010. The chances are that his loyalists have already been deployed to carry out this project.

Even so, Mugabe faces other obstacles to any attempt to prolong his stay. Aside from his opponents within his party, he must now contend with the hint of an emerging consensus between Africa and the west over his future. Both the African Union and the Southern African Development Community (SADC) have become more concentrated on developing a post-Mugabe dispensation. In the light of a growing rift in Mugabe's power base, officials in Pretoria feel more confident of building consensus for its policy of "quiet diplomacy".

Regional sensitivities persist around the delicate matter of being "told what to do about Zimbabwe". But the broader picture has changed. Widespread civic criticisms of the Mugabe regime, in Africa and at global level, have eroded the pretensions of the Zimbabwean leader in portraying himself as someone prepared to challenge the West.

An opposition in trouble

In the national context, opposition forces remain vulnerable. Notwithstanding the moral stature they have gained, both factions of the divided Movement for Democratic Change have suffered from severe state harassment, violence and infiltration since the late 1990s. The legacy of the split within the MDC endures, alongside more recent attempts at coordination. Both sides need a new direction to restore morale.

A new sense of hope in the possibility of change would encourage more unified action. A revived opposition would be a key element in any move towards a new politics of "transition", and the likely beneficiary of any attempt to open the media. In such an expanded political space, the remaining legitimacy of ZANU-PF would be sorely tested.

By October 2007, it had become apparent that opposition factions are not yet capable of unity. The divisions between the two formations have hardened and taken on a depressingly ethnic dimension, once again drawing the MDC into the past habits of nationalist politics. The political situation in Zimbabwe remains extremely difficult. The only winner in this divided politics is likely to be ZANU-PF.

In the light of these processes, South Africa and the Southern African Development Community (SADC) will seek to protect the integrity of African ownership of any initiative on Zimbabwe. Regional leaders will be wary of suggestions that they are "doing the bidding of the West", and continued support for Mugabe by strong voices within the SADC will constrain their actions. The SADC summit in Lusaka in August 2007 confirmed this trend, with the organisation still tethered to its official position of solidarity with Mugabe.

No matter what private criticisms may be made on the extent of Mugabe's political delinquency, the emphasis will be on "a soft transition" to accommodate Zimbabwe's leader. The feasibility of this approach must be judged against the recalcitrance of entrenched forces in ZANU-PF. If the SADC initiative fails, the most likely alternative is continued deterioration of the Zimbabwean crisis.

Brian Raftopoulos *is former professor of development studies at the University of Zimbabwe. He is director of research and advocacy for the Solidarity Peace Trust, a Zimbabwean non-governmental organisation, based in Cape Town.*

A new ZANU-PF is not enough

The foundations of democracy in Zimbabwe have been eroded by corruption, patronage and violence. Nobody should pretend they will be restored merely by reforming ZANU-PF, writes **Arthur Mutambara**, *leader of the breakaway faction of the opposition Movement for Democratic Change.*

There has been a lot of debate and discussion about the succession issue in ZANU-PF. In some quarters, the possibility of a ZANU-PF successor to Mugabe has been lauded as the key to unlocking the Zimbabwean crisis, while others have postulated a reformed ZANU-PF as the answer to our national challenges. There is speculation that some key players in South Africa would prefer a reformed ZANU-PF government with or without the opposition as a junior partner.

The international community, particularly western governments, have shown a keen interest in the jockeying for positions among ZANU-PF factions, which seems to imply that if any one of the factions were to successfully replace Mugabe – by whatever method – they would consider normalising relationships with Zimbabwe. The thinking seems to be that the problem is Robert Mugabe the person, and that anyone else will do just fine.

First and foremost, the Zimbabwean crisis is bigger than the person of Robert Mugabe. Over the past 27 years, ZANU-PF has developed a distinct socio-politico-economic culture and value system rooted in political illegitimacy, poor country governance, economic mismanagement, bad policies, corruption, patronage, incompetence and disrespect for the rule of law. Whilst Mugabe is the personification and cardinal symbol of this misrule, these traits are now deeply rooted within ZANU-PF, which is rotten to the core. Mugabe is the glue that keeps the rot together.

Dismantling this oppressive system and creating a peaceful, democratic and prosperous Zimbabwe require more than the demise of Robert Mugabe as a political player. There are many individuals and institutions linked to ZANU-PF that are benefiting from the status quo. They seek to continue milking this patronage system with or without Mugabe. It is highly unlikely that ZANU-PF will operate differently when he goes. None of the potential Mugabe successors in any of the factions or sub-factions has articulated a different value system, institutional framework or strategic vision. They have no transformative agenda. Their value proposition is simply that they are not Robert Mugabe. Beyond that it is business as usual.

How can those in the international community, including South Africans, that claim to cherish values of democracy, freedom and economic prosperity even entertain or fathom such a perverted succession? We hope we are not witnessing those treacherous tendencies towards double standards, hypocrisy and duplicity. A reformed ZANU-PF succession strategy must be rejected purely on the grounds of principles and values. The ANC and PAC freedom fighters would not accept a reformed apartheid framework. Jewish freedom fighters would not accept alliances with factions of the Nazi regime. Zimbabweans should not sell their souls on the altar of convenience and compromise.

We seek a total institutional and structural revolution rooted in radical transformation of our political value system. This is simply impossible under a ZANU-PF successor.

A credible opposition?

Confronted by a crumbling administration, the Movement for Democratic Change has failed to articulate a compelling alternative. The ruling party sustains an illusion of democracy, writes **Joram Nyathi**, *while the MDC wants others' failures to revive its fortunes.*

Surveying the raft of problems in Zimbabwe today, one can safely claim that no nation in the region is more ripe for a change of leadership. Daily life is blighted by crippling shortages of power, fuel, drugs and basic commodities. As I write, official inflation is over 7,634% and unemployment is close to 80%. The explanation for the prolonged suffering lies not only in the failures of the ruling ZANU-PF party, but also the opposition Movement for Democratic Change led by the redoubtable trade-unionist-turned-politician, Morgan Tsvangirai.

There is no question that President Robert Mugabe is an astute political schemer in his own right, never more so than when confronted with challenges to his hold on power. In rural constituencies, Mugabe has proved adept at deceiving villagers by appearing to accord them power to choose leaders which in fact they don't have. Most of the candidates they are asked to endorse are selected by the party leadership.

The cancer of political patronage has spread so widely that none in ZANU-PF is clean enough to openly challenge Mugabe for the leadership. Yet the president himself is not necessarily corrupt in any specific sense. Rather, he has allowed those around him to make fabulous riches in circumstances so murky that they have, by their own actions, compromised their ability to oppose him.

Mugabe has obliquely chided corrupt officials, exploiting these venal tendencies to his advantage. In both the ruling party and the government, threat of exposure has become a constant danger to his henchmen – although Mugabe has taken no action to stamp out corruption. Consequently, dissent within the party rarely rises above the occasional murmur. The scope for any meaningful competition of ideas or policies has been drastically reduced.

Missed opportunities

For Zimbabwe's opposition, confronted by this monolithic and almost moribund party machine, one might expect ZANU-PF to represent a soft and slow-moving target. The MDC has the people and the world on its side, yet its advance on State House has been perpetually frustrated.

The party has lost the moral high ground since it split over whether to contest elections to the Senate in October 2005. Mugabe frequently characterises his opponents as agents of imperialist forces. Indecision has reduced the MDC to its weakest point since the party was launched in September 1999.

Among the most striking examples of this political naïveté was the presidential election in 2002. People were shocked by the outcome. Tsvangirai lost under questionable circumstances: he called it "daylight robbery". But when asked what action he would take, the MDC leader merely responded that the people would decide.

The opportunity for Tsvangirai was real, and despite a show of strength by the military there was evidence of nervousness in government. Mugabe left the country on a convenient trip to Malaysia. Subsequently he recovered his nerve and played his cards well by pretending that he was interested in holding talks with the opposition. An agenda was agreed to address the deepening economic crisis and the issue of Mugabe's legitimacy. South African observers endorsed the ballot, after President Thabo Mbeki accepted assurances from both sides that they would meet to find common ground.

Without any call to protest from the MDC's leadership, people became accustomed to the "stolen" result, while Tsvangirai pursued his case in court. Since then, the case has been mothballed in the legal system – the verdict will be of no more than academic interest. Once the temperature had cooled, Mugabe felt secure enough to abandon the charade of negotiations.

Another missed opportunity for the opposition was "Operation *Murambatsvina*", the widely condemned clearance of "unofficial" settlements in poor suburbs in May 2005. With their homes and livelihoods destroyed, critics have speculated that MDC supporters were again ready to be mobilised into action. The poor were already in the streets: they had nothing to lose but their chains. Once again, the MDC's real trouble was a lack of political leadership to match the president's cunning. Leadership failed.

An enduring problem is that precious little is known about the MDC's policies. The last we heard about its "RESTART" programme was during the 2005 election campaign, in which the party fared badly. Since then, the political and economic situation has deteriorated. Time has rendered the prescriptions of "RESTART" almost anachronistic.

Instead of building a united front, MDC leaders of both factions have tended to go into denial about the impact of the rift which caused the party to split in 2005. Attempts at decisive action, which might have regained the confidence of voters nationwide, have been spoiled by attempts to play the ethnic card – just as Mugabe plays the race card when it suits him.

Election prospects

There is no doubt that Tsvangirai enjoys wide support in urban areas and across all social strata. The poor have turned to him because Mugabe's land reforms have left them hungry. The rich look on him favourably because government policies have hurt or destroyed their businesses. Much of this support is a default reaction against the hopeless ineptitude of ZANU-PF.

The MDC remains vulnerable in the countryside, where it has failed to penetrate rural constituencies. With the sole exception of Matabeleland in 2000, the MDC has never won a rural seat where the majority of constituencies are located. There is a tendency in the media – wrongly, in my view – to describe this territory as a stronghold for ZANU-PF. Unless the MDC can accept fair criticism of its shortcomings, it looks set to remain in opposition.

And Mugabe may hold on well beyond elections scheduled for March 2008. In September 2007, parliament passed Constitutional Amendment 18 with the support of both MDC factions. The proposals, tabled by ZANU-PF in the wake of regional mediation between both parties, will increase the number of constituencies in 2008 from 150 to 210. The number of Senate seats will rise from 60 to 84. Critics of the MDC stance fear the new constitutencies will create new opportunities for gerrymandering by Mugabe, such that ZANU-PF may emerge from the election with a stronger majority.

If the president has any plans to step down, he is determined to do so on his own terms. At the last ZANU-PF conference in December 2006, party members rejected

Mugabe's proposal to extend his term to 2010. Since then the MDC has adopted a more conciliatory tone, rallying behind Constitutional Amendment 18 and speculating on ways of "accommodating" reformist elements who support democratic change. For a party which seeks to speak to the future, the MDC finds itself in the invidious position of courting break-away elements in ZANU-PF to buttress its cause.

The ruling party conference in December 2007 will give a clear indication of Mugabe's hold on his own party. In the event that "elements" within the ruling party – led by either retired army general Solomon Mujuru or Emmerson Mnangagwa, minister of rural housing – succeed in blocking Mugabe's candidature next year, his successor may favour cooperation with the MDC.

One possible outcome, strongly favoured by South Africa, is the emergence of a government of national unity. Yet again, this would entail the MDC reacting to an initiative from ZANU-PF – in this instance with encouragement from the Southern African Development Community (SADC).

South African president Thabo Mbeki has brokered talks between the two parties, but there is no doubt that ZANU-PF would still occupy a commanding position. According to Justice minister Patrick Chinamasa strategists for ZANU-PF anticipate that the rift in the MDC will divide its supporters at the polls. Chinamasa predicted the MDC would emerge so badly wounded from elections in 2008 that he saw no need for negotiations.

Meanwhile, the MDC has yet to confirm whether it intends to participate in the joint parliamentary and presidential elections scheduled for March 2008. It is not much of a choice. Boycotting the poll would scupper any hope of defining a new political agenda for Zimbabwe in the near future, yet without thorough reform of electoral law and institutions, participating in elections would only legitimise a controversial ZANU-PF victory.

To date, the MDC's best chance of reaching power is likely to rest not on its own abilities, but on the aptitude of ZANU-PF to navigate a new path through the, as yet unknown, territory of Zimbabwe after Mugabe.

Joram Nyathi *is deputy editor of the* Zimbabwe Independent.

Calling in the generals

Mugabe has deployed the army against opponents of his regime and rewarded officers with new opportunities for patronage and profit. Elements of the military have committed human rights abuses, but many more are disillusioned. **Martin Rupiya**, *a former lieutenant colonel in the Zimbabwe National Army, argues that soldiers cannot resolve a political crisis.*

As the political crisis in Zimbabwe deteriorates, a number of seasoned political commentators and actors have speculated publicly on the likely consequences of intervention by the military. Among the veiled references to a forced removal of the incumbents from office, I shall quote only the following:

> *Generals may be the ones who could pull Zimbabwe through...*
> – *Jonathan Moyo*

> *'Better the devil we know' is the only practical deal possible...*
> – *Trevor Ncube*

> *Militarism is the fundamental problem in Zimbabwe's political culture [and therefore no solution is possible without the military]...*
> – *Ibbo Mandaza*[1]

The background to the call is understandable: a society is disintegrating while the ruling elite behave as if oblivious to the destruction. For those with a clear understanding of the economic situation, an urgent solution is required. In their view, little will be left of Zimbabwe if the country continues on its current route until elections in 2008. The "last scenario" of a military coup has gained ground in discussion of Zimbabwe's future.

However, any invitation for the military to seize political power lacks a conceptual understanding of military coups on the African continent and diverts attention from the responsibilities of political leaders. The call for military intervention ignores the impact of Zimbabwe's crisis on the capacity and professionalism of the army, police and state security organisations. Lower and middle-ranking personnel have abandoned these organisations in droves, deterred by poor conditions of service and the personal cost of operating in a highly politicised environment in which they continually come into contact with citizens who have suffered state-sponsored repression. Defections have left the military divided, severely damaged and its reputation tarnished. Any attempt to assume a political role would likely be the final nail in the coffin of a barely functional institution. Proponents of military intervention largely ignore the urgent need for a u-turn in security policy to restore credibility, and the related problem of how to negotiate an exit strategy for a return to barracks.

Theorists identify three types of military coup, all familiar in Africa:

- *A Breakthrough coup* – generally carried out by junior or Non-Commissioned Officers (NCOs): a violent and often chaotic break with the past, ushering in a new bureaucracy.
- *A Guardian coup* – often described as "musical chairs", avoiding any fundamental restructuring in power relations: often led by senior officers acting with political elites; power may alternate between military and civilian authorities.
- *A Veto coup* – when the army vetoes mass participation to repress broad-based opposition, often as a direct result of an invitation to the army to intervene in politics.

To all intents and purposes, on January 9th 2002 the military carried out a veto coup in Zimbabwe. A phalanx of senior commanders appeared on television to announce the criteria for any candidate aspiring to presidential office – a so-called "straight jacket" of conditions which specifically excluded opposition leader Morgan Tsvangirai. Since then, soldiers have emerged at the helm of key public enterprises to wield substantial political patronage. Proponents of further intervention by the military ignore the fact that the scenario they advocate has already occurred.

A partisan military?

Armies have often been touted as instruments for modernisation where state and liberal democratic institutions have failed. In underdeveloped states, a military coup may maintain a semblance of sovereignty while facilitating change. The organisation, culture and discipline of a military force, under a clearly defined chain of command, mean that armies are equipped to respond in times of crisis.[2]

President Robert Mugabe has said that Zimbabwe is "at war". Since the elections of June 2000, opposition supporters have been designated as the "enemy" and as proxies of foreign power. National security strategy has shifted from the benign 1980s policy of national reconciliation, towards a more offensive posture. As the main instrument of this policy, soldiers have been pitted against all elements of society which do not, openly and explicitly, support the ruling party. In this context, the state has publicly condoned violent action against its opponents. The state has chosen arbitrary justice and coercion over the rule of law. To this end, the military has been restructured and its role redefined to include coercion and enforcement of presidential *fiat*.

At the command level, key military personnel are dominated by the former leadership of the Zimbabwe African National Liberation Army (ZANLA), the guerrilla army led by Mugabe during the colonial war in Rhodesia. These personnel remained "a central and dominant feature in the Zimbabwean state," observes Ibbo Mandaza, a political analyst with close ties to ZANU-PF. At the same time, the military repression under the incumbent government does not include *all* elements of the military and security sectors. There is strong evidence that the coercive capacity of the state is controlled by elements from the intelligence services, police, army and civil service, sometimes doubling as senior party officials.

A recalcitrant regime needs only a few thousand personnel to undertake massive repression. Many atrocities orchestrated by the ruling political party have been committed by small numbers of personnel co-opted by security chiefs, leaving the majority of the forces in limbo. In the event of a coup, this small element would be acting *against* a majority of the police, military and prison service, which has so far remained neutral.

In early 2002, when the generals announced their "straight jacket" of conditions for presidential candidates, Mozambican president Joaquim Chissano warned on behalf of the Southern African Development Community (SADC) that Zimbabwe's military should beware of interfering in politics. In the intervening period, senior officers have played a decisive political role as members of the Joint Operational Command (JOC) in collaboration with members of the ruling party. However, they have, quite rightly, continued to play second fiddle to politicians.

Among soldiers deployed to civilian or professional posts, a significant proportion occupy vacancies left by the mass exodus of skilled and experienced tradesmen. Soldiers have emerged as a necessary stopgap to fill professional posts running the railways, the Grain Marketing Board and utilities such as energy, water and electricity. They are the wrong people for these jobs, making it unlikely – for as long as military officers are in charge – that these institutions will find interest among financial and technical investors.

In a "war" economy, day-to-day decisions made by soldiers respond to a tight hierarchy of command, rather than market forces or new opportunities. Consequently, banks and other financial institutions have been reluctant to extend funding to public enterprises under the direct control of the military. Specialist skills are urgently required before the economy grinds to a halt.

Over and above their role in parastatal corporations, the military have been saddled with a new responsibility of managing both new extra-military groups such as the National Service, the openly politically aligned War Veterans Reserve, and Traditional Chiefs in the rural areas.

Much of the military leadership, and a majority of the rank and file, are ripe for retirement at the first opportunity. The average age of a young cadre signing up at a ZANLA Assembly Point during the ceasefire, which preceded democratic elections in 1980, was about 20 years old. After 27 years of independence, these men and women are approaching their 50s and early 60s. Under their conditions of service, many are beyond retirement age but were prevented from leaving by new regulations after Zimbabwe intervened in the war-torn Democratic Republic of Congo.

As the domestic economy contracted, others have stayed on merely for the opportunities and patronage available to military personnel. Senior soldiers have been among the beneficiaries of the redistribution of land, with access to scarce commodities and public assets. For some, military duties have become an unwanted chore as they divide their time between uniformed activities and the pursuit of farming or business operations with the tacit approval of the state. A small coterie of soldiers have become serious entrepreneurs and significant stakeholders in the economy. These roles will need to be reviewed in the event that the crisis comes to an end.

Running on empty

Military capacity has been severely degraded by economic recession and the effects of "targeted" international sanctions imposed since 2000, while troops were active in the Democratic Republic of Congo. Zimbabwe has lacked resources to buy arms or fund higher officer training programmes. A siege mentality has emerged, often resonating with the feeling of victim-hood and persecution articulated by politicians. This has drawn the military closer to the ruling party, compounding a belief that economic sanctions are merely an example of imperial machinations by Britain and its allies. These sentiments may be an unintended consequence of international sanctions, but they are causing soldiers to act against opponents of ZANU-PF and anyone identified as a proxy for opposition interests.

Evidence presented to parliamentary committees indicates that troops are owed money in unpaid allowances, lack adequate accommodation and training facilities, and suffer from a shortage of equipment. Fuel allowances restrict training of air force personnel to a maximum eights weeks' flying per year. Besides the trying conditions of service, the professionalism achieved at great cost since 1980 has been undermined by the politicisation of military command and control. I have established from conversations with military officials in neighbouring states that many SADC governments are now wary of their troops undertaking joint activities with the politically involved Zimbabwe Defence Forces. Disillusioned officers have quit their posts without tendering a formal resignation or waiting to be discharged. In my view, the security sector in Zimbabwe may actually have experienced greater adverse effects of the political crisis than most other sectors of society, albeit largely unacknowledged.

A relationship under strain

The political elite is angry and vindictive: politicians will not suffer any sleepless nights as a result of orders issued to the military to enforce actions which would not stand up to legal scrutiny. A culture of impunity has characterised the hostilities in Zimbabwe, and this will need to be addressed in order to deter perpetrators of violence.

The professional credentials of Zimbabwe's military have been sullied, under the gaze of their peers in other security institutions across southern Africa and beyond. For an organisation with an impressive track record, gained under fire in three regional conflicts, this is a severe setback. Zimbabwean troops were active throughout the 1980s in the Mozambican conflict (until 1992), in Lesotho in 1998, and more recently in the Democratic Republic of Congo. Since 2002, the Zimbabwean military has been conscious of a changed role as pawn in a domestic political game.

In December 2006, Chief of Defence Staff General C. Chiwenga appealed to "political leaders to sort out the political and economic crisis, as soldiers wished to avoid seeing the day when they have to turn their weapons against their own citizens." The recognition of such a prospect by the country's top soldier acknowledged the strain imposed on the relationship between the ruling party, the military as an institution, and the rest of the society. In this regard atrocities and human rights abuses, committed by elements of the military, will – in the wake of the current crisis – need to be considered for pardons or special amnesty. Precedents for amnesty can be found in the end of the independence struggle, 1979-1980, and the dispensation granted in 1988 to soldiers active in Matabeleland.

In spite, or because, of abuses imposed by the adoption of a partisan national security strategy, the military retains the staunch backing of the ruling elite. Herein lies a conundrum for those political commentators who assume the political elite is becoming hostage to the military class. The politicians are very much in charge. Their policy of deploying military force as a political instrument to suppress opposition culminated, in August 2007, in a series of public accolades and commendations by Mugabe during the Heroes Day celebrations. This places the responsibility for resolving Zimbabwe's crisis squarely in the political arena.

Calls for the military to take over are therefore misplaced. The main obstacle to resolving Zimbabwe's crisis is the stance of political recalcitrants, determined to pursue their partisan campaign by military and coercive means. The national security strategy adopted by Mugabe, for the purposes of "war", has degraded Zimbabwean institutions and led to acute suffering by ordinary people. With the mediation and intervention of the SADC, this abuse of national security strategy must be addressed. The more rabid elements of the military can be granted amnesty and retired from service. At this point, soldiers will return to barracks.

Martin Rupiya *is director of the Institute for Security Studies in Pretoria, South Africa. He previously served as a lieutenant colonel in the Zimbabwe National Army.*

A bad case
of writer's block

Caine Prize winner **Brian Chikwava** *believes politicians have much to learn from writers of fiction. Zimbabwe's leaders lack the imagination to salvage their script.*

To a man who has only a hammer, every problem that he encounters looks like a nail.

So said the American psychologist Abraham Maslow – and, being a writer, I find myself in a similar position. I happen to have only a pen, and every problem that crosses my path resembles a story in need of fixing.

The art of story-writing has a lot in common with the art of politics.

A glance at Zimbabwe tells me that this is a bad story. It needs more than tough editing: it needs a complete rewrite. Whether the script can be fixed depends not just on its main protagonist, Robert Mugabe, but also on the opposition. Their part is to put new ideas on the table, to carry the story in another direction.

Mugabe believes he is living an historical epic, something like *War & Peace*. Except that his story is packed with more heroic exploits than Tolstoy's, and can end only with the triumph of his will over history. Many others think it should be shelved under "tragedy".

Mugabe has scripted himself into a role where there is no room for fresh thinking. If a *mhondoro* spirit (the mythic lion spirits that are the custodians of the people) were to appear before him with an offer to give the president anything he desired, but on condition that this wish shall be given twice to every citizen, it would not be out of character now for Mugabe to ask that one of his eyes be gouged out.

This is a failure of imagination. But it also reflects a failure of the opposition to articulate a vision of its own. Nowhere was this better illustrated than after Morgan Tsvangirai's brutal assault at the hands of the police. Tsvangirai's wounds were paraded on television stations worldwide – the veritable victim. I am not suggesting that Tsvangirai should not feel pain, nor indeed that he is not a victim. What I seek to understand is how the people are supposed to reconcile this sorry spectacle with the inspiration required of an indomitable and populist leader?

For his part, Mugabe probably suffers sleepless nights and fierce headaches. But we have yet to hear about that. In an age where the art of image-making is mastered even by teenagers on MySpace.com, it seems odd that Tsvangirai has not grasped this.

Or maybe the problem is deeper than that. Tsvangirai has two audiences, after all. One is outside Zimbabwe, to whom he must look like a victim. The other is inside Zimbabwe, where he must act the part of irrepressible opposition leader. He is not sure if he's a victim or a fighter.

With a trade union background, one would have expected Tsvangirai's Movement for Democratic Change to speak a language that inspires the common people. Instead he has flirted with neo-liberal policies. The opposition do not know if they are free-marketeers or a grassroots movement. There is no language to convey an alternative political project, while Mugabe has been able to pose as a people's leader, monopolising the idiom of the Left – with all its Leftist language.

This may explain why Tsvangirai, given a chance to script a new plot for Zimbabwe, is still holding his pen mid-air. A better story lies somewhere inside his head, but he does not have the words to tell it. Staring at a blank sheet of paper, Tsvangirai must decide whether his character is hero or victim.

Extracted from an article first published in the *Mail & Guardian*, May 4th 2007, and edited for clarity.

2. ECONOMY AND LAND

The war on prices

Legislation to promote indigenous ownership and a price freeze are among the measures adopted by Mugabe's government to contain the worst economic crisis in the country's history. Ministers have blamed international sanctions for a chronic shortage of foreign exchange, while inflows of hard currency from tobacco and other exports have dwindled. **Nothando Ndebele** *looks for lessons from Germany and Bolivia as Zimbabwe fights a losing battle against hyperinflation.*

There is inflation, high inflation and then there is hyperinflation. The first is acceptable, the second worrying and the third is a sheer nightmare. A country is usually classified as having hyperinflation when the monthly inflation rate is greater than 50%. By July 2007, official data showed Zimbabwe's inflation rate at a staggering 7,635%, at a time when most developing economies in Africa have brought inflation down to double-digit levels and many can boast single-digit inflation.

In the classic economists' definition, high inflation is caused by "too much money chasing too few goods". Hyperinflation is usually triggered by a rapid growth in the supply of paper money, as governments attempt to pay their bills by printing more money under the auspices of the central bank. Printing new bank notes produces reams of new cash to fund debt repayments, civil service wages, defence spending and "undisclosed" expenditures.

It's a vicious circle. Printing new cash increases the total supply of money in the economy, leading to more competition for goods, which in turn pushes up prices. In order to cover expenditure for the same quantity of goods, government has to print more money. People rush to buy goods today to avoid paying higher prices tomorrow. This accelerating demand pushes prices still higher into the realm of hyperinflation. People lose faith in money as the purchasing power of every banknote falls.

Victims of hyperinflation are all those whose income cannot keep up with the rise in prices of goods and services. Unless wages keep pace with rising prices, salaried people become impoverished. In effect, printing money as a means to finance government expenditure becomes an added "tax burden" on the population.

Beneficiaries of hyperinflation tend to be speculators. If you have a warehouse full of inventory, holding on to it today will earn you a higher price tomorrow. Consumers, meanwhile, knowing that a loaf of bread costing $1 today could sell for $1.30 tomorrow, want to buy as much bread as they can today. It is easy to see why periods of hyperinflation are often accompanied by periods of civil unrest.

Lessons from history

How do we work ourselves out of this situation? Zimbabwe is not the first country to suffer from the ravages of hyperinflation. Germany experienced a period of hyperinflation after the First World War. More recently, in 1985, Bolivia witnessed a period of severe hyperinflation which peaked at 12,000%. At its height, the Bolivian government funded about 93% of its monthly expenses with newly printed money. Both Germany and Bolivia conquered the beast and restored stability to prices and the economy.

In Germany, the government created a new unit of currency whose value was linked to a tangible asset – in this case, the price of gold. Banknotes could be converted to gold on demand. This restored value in the currency and brought confidence that the government was committed to halting the supply of money. I doubt this would be sufficient in Zimbabwe today, at least without a change of leadership. A "wait-and-see approach" would be viewed with great scepticism, even in the unlikely event that Zimbabwe's Reserve Bank has sufficient gold reserves to defend the currency.

A more plausible alternative is that Zimbabwe will have no choice but to adopt the Bolivian tactic of shock treatment under a new government. It is not called "shock treatment" for nothing: Bolivia simultaneously removed all price controls and froze payrolls to curb expenditure. The first policy removed incentives for speculators to hoard inventories in the knowledge that prices were certain to rise over time – thus it reduced constraints on the supply of goods. The second policy – amounting to a pledge by the government to live within its means – removed the need to print new money.

This two-pronged policy was crucial to Bolivia's success in taming hyperinflation. Only with an unambiguous stance by the government were people willing to believe that the government was committed to improving their livelihoods. Without buy-in from the people, the government would have struggled to sustain tough fiscal discipline.

War on prices

The issue of credibility is the first obstacle to the "tailor-made" solutions for hyperinflation which have been proposed by Mugabe's government, culminating in the so-called "War on Prices". Slashing of prices to what the government has determined as "affordable" and "reasonable" levels has been accompanied by a propaganda campaign centred on the "evil profiteering of the business community at the expense of the ordinary citizen." This has occurred with no mention of the government's printing of money or of exorbitant expenditures left to run unabated.

How the new prices were arrived at, and what calculations of supply and demand simulations were used to determine the economic impact, remain a mystery. What we know for sure is that manufacturers and retailers have been forced to deliver and sell goods at prices below their input costs. It does not take a rocket scientist to realise that few, if any, rational individuals will produce goods for 10 cents if they are only allowed to sell them for 5 cents. Zimbabweans as a whole are numerate and even the informal trader selling tomatoes by the bus-stop knows the difference between profit and loss.

The result, naturally, has been the proliferation of empty shelves. Instead of meat, the refrigerators in the butchery sections of some supermarkets have been loaded with vegetables. These shortages will continue, exacerbated by a recently revised list of restrictions on imports of food and foodstuffs. Many families depend on monthly grocery packages from relatives and friends sent from South Africa and Botswana. Until August 2007, the process of sending food to Zimbabwe was fairly easy. Since then, packages of bananas or oranges require an import licence – although how strictly the new laws will be enforced in the privileged suburbs of Beitbridge and Plumtree remains to be seen.

This approach to price controls and import restrictions is yet another example of "tailor made" policies in Zimbabwe defying economic logic. The War on Prices has led to shortages, while imports which could fill the gap are restricted. How does the government plan to feed the nation? Poor economic policies have been compounded by disappointing harvests. Anecdotal reports suggest stocks held by the Grain Marketing Board have diminished. Several global agencies which monitor famine and food shortages around the world have warned of an impending food crisis in Zimbabwe, especially in the southwest and urban areas.

Inevitably, these shortages have brought escalating prices in the parallel market. Some estimates put inflation in the black market as high as 20,000%. The shortages have brought increasing desperation. On August 15th 2007, a security guard and a young child were killed in a stampede in Bulawayo. People had heard rumours of an impending delivery which resulted in a frenzied storming of a truck carrying sugar.

A recovery plan
Most Zimbabweans understand that the current state of affairs is unsustainable. However, the biggest contribution to price stability must come from the government and its public sector. Given that Zimbabwe is currently running a budget deficit in excess of 40% of gross domestic product, there needs to be large rationalisation of government departments. I would suggest we start with the army – who needs all those soldiers and defence equipment? Next, parastatals such as PTC (post and telecommunications) and the electricity company could be partially or fully privatised to raise funds and improve efficiency.

Would the Bolivian remedy work in Zimbabwe? In late August 2007, the government published new laws to regulate prices and salaries. The state-owned *Herald* newspaper reported that it is now forbidden for anyone in the private and public sectors to raise salaries, wages, rents or service charges without official permission. This is a step, albeit roughly, in the right direction.

I am doubtful about how strictly the government can adhere to such measures. Will the ruling ZANU-PF have the mettle to resist pressure from public servants – including the army, war veterans and the police – for higher wages? As for the private sector, evidence from other countries shows that controlling prices in this arena is difficult. In general, it takes a reduction in inflation expectations to secure the intended results.

Nor should we under-estimate the extent of the social shock which accompanied the Bolivian therapy. At first, this could include an upward spike in inflation for basic commodities, such as fuel, which have been controlled at prices well below black market rates. The combination of higher prices and zero wage growth would curtail demand, resulting in a stabilisation of prices – less money chasing more expensive goods. The poor would bear the brunt of these economic adjustments.

To alleviate the adverse effects of much needed reform, the government should simultaneously adopt policies to secure improved access to foreign exchange. These include:

- A revival of the agricultural sector: agriculture is important both for domestic consumption and the generation of foreign exchange – Zimbabwe has produced well qualified graduates in agriculture who, together with farmers, know what is required to improve productivity.
- Resuscitate the manufacturing sector: a lack of foreign exchange has stunted growth in recent years, despite the fact that Zimbabwe boasts a highly educated and flexible labour force.
- Adopt a more efficient trade regime: bottlenecks and impediments to trade need to be removed; simplification of duties and tariffs will stabilise prices and help to bring down the cost of goods.
- Emphasise tourism: this is a quick route to foreign exchange and job creation, with benefits across the services industry – Zambia and South Africa have benefited from the demise of tourism in Zimbabwe over the last decade; political stability would help us to recover this lost but lucrative market.

In the longer term, a reform-minded government will have to set its own house in order. The tax department is said to be planning a large overhaul and restructuring of its activities – not before time. Tax revenues are slipping away amid the general confusion, and these need to be brought to book. There are good lessons to be learnt from the success of the South African Revenue Service. I look forward to the day when Zimbabwe's finance minister is faced with the same problem as his South African counterpart, Trevor Manuel, of significantly higher than expected tax revenues. How better to spend it than on health, education and development? By a government which has not had to print a single note for any of it.

Nothando Ndebele *is a Zimbabwean economist and executive director of Renaissance Specialist Fund Managers in Cape Town.*

Then and now

Redistribution of land has tackled the legacy of racial privilege, creating many more medium-sized plots. In this excerpt from an article for the Mail & Guardian *newspaper,* **Sam Moyo** *argues that while land ownership has become more democratic, a new dispensation has spawned new inequalities.*[1]

The distribution of land has been unjust and in need of redress. Whites and corporate landowners held about 4,000 farms, each averaging more than 2,000 hectares. By 2000, policy and laws, markets and international intervention had failed adequately to change this.

A generation of young graduates could not find meaningful jobs. Income and wealth inequalities grew. As wages slumped, the agricultural sector became more dependent on erratic external financing and aid.

Small farmers had been bolstered in the 1980s by state intervention and the regulation of agricultural markets. But as labour conditions deteriorated, food security was put at risk. Problems of rural and urban landlessness intensified, leading to a revived politics of land reclamation – and, since 1997, opposition to it.

Redistribution has redressed some of the imbalances of the legacy of racially skewed land ownership. But it has spawned new inequalities, as well as challenges from former landowners.

Reforms extended access to land to more than 150,000 families and significantly downsized the average size of commercial landholdings. About 12,000 new medium scale farm units now exist with an average of 200 hectares each. More than 120,000 beneficiary families hold less than 100 hectares each.

This new dispensation sits side-by-side with aspects of the old. Approximately 4,000 landholders own farms of about 700 hectares each. These include foreign landholders, large agro-industrial corporate estates, individual white farmers and old and new black farmers.

Although a significant number of former white farmers and enterprises remain, the future of white landownership remains contested. At the same time, substantial numbers of Zimbabwe's peasants, women and labourers object that they have been excluded from the redistribution.

Less than 10% of the land beneficiaries are former farm-workers. There are still 200,000 agricultural workers, most of whom continue to reside as farm tenants on redistributed land, without secure land rights.

In broad terms, access and ownership have been democratised. This must be weighed against the continued politicisation of land reform, by both ruling and oppositional forces.

The main impact of reform has been to transform agrarian social and labour relations. The reforms increased the degree to which farms are self-operated or family-operated, some of which use hired labour. But the slump in agricultural production, by about 50% since 2001, has also reduced the number of full-time agricultural jobs. Wages have fallen, and payment can be irregular.

The causes of this decline are keenly debated in Zimbabwe.

Production of the staple maize crop, for instance, suffered severely, not because of land transfers but due to the frequent droughts and a scarcity of essential inputs such as fertiliser.

Tobacco, wheat and oilseed production declined due to reduced areas planted on the transferred land, limited financing of new farmers and their limited skills.

Loss and withdrawal of farm machinery and irrigation equipment affected plantings for most crops. The rate of livestock production fell as a result of rapid slaughtering and rustling of cattle, limited breeding stocks and a shortage of skills.

The reduction of agro-industrial inputs, largely because of foreign exchange shortages and price controls, affected production of all crops. International sanctions on Zimbabwe also hurt the sector.

Reversal of the land redistribution is not politically feasible, but sustainable use of land will require key changes in agricultural and economic policy.

The whole process of land distribution needs to be concluded and compensation for land improvements speeded up.

The first priority is to approach reform with a consistency that has been lacking. A new agrarian strategy must focus on improving the livelihoods of the majority. If the policies are supportive, smallholders can play a critical role in the future of Zimbabwean farming.

Extracted from the *Mail & Guardian* newspaper, April 20th 2007, and edited for clarity.

How many farms is enough?

Attempts to empower rural populations made more progress in the first decade of independence than in all the decades since, writes **Phillan Zamchiya**. *The "Fast Track" redistribution of land has brought hardship, famine and risk of further unrest.*

Zimbabwe's "Fast Track" land reform has not led to a more egalitarian nor more democratic ownership of land. In the words of veteran nationalist Eddison Zvobgo: "We have tainted what was a glorious revolution, reducing it to some agrarian racist enterprise."

At the birth of Zimbabwe in 1980, about 6,000 white farmers owned 15.5 million hectares of land. Indigenous communities farmed 16.4 million hectares.[1] In the first decade of majority rule, the government embarked on a pro-poor approach to land reform with the aim of reducing poverty and pre-empting potential causes of rural unrest.

By 1989, the government was able to resettle 48,000 households, despite the restrictions of a constitutional clause that required all transfers to be negotiated – in hard currency – on a willing buyer / willing seller basis.[2] With the help of seeds, fertiliser and services provided by state institutions, cotton and maize production by smallholders increased sharply.

According to the British High Commission in Harare, the UK provided £47m for land reform between 1980-1985: £20m in the form of a Land Resettlement Grant and £27m in budgetary support to help the Zimbabwean government's own contribution to the programme.[3]

The influence of the International Monetary Fund, under an Economic Structural Adjustment Facility, and the interests of emerging indigenous elites caused the government's focus to shift in the early 1990s. The objective of agrarian policy was revised, away from attaining a more equal society and towards supporting the creation of more efficient agrarian capitalism.[4] As a consequence, only 71,000 households had been re-settled by 1997.[5]

State support measures introduced in the first decade of majority rule were withdrawn, mainly because land reform came lower on the agenda of the government than neo-liberal economic reforms. The Land Resettlement Grant was closed in 1996 with £3m unspent.[6]

In 1998, the government convened a conference on land reform among donors. Multilateral institutions and international donors endorsed a two-year programme, which was disturbed by the farm invasions in early 2000.

The emotive issue of land reform was revived by the government as popular support for ZANU-PF waned in response to economic hardship. Soon after the rejection of the February 2000 referendum on a draft constitution, government-sponsored militias began to occupy mainly white commercial farms. About 4,000 white commercial farmers were violently evicted in the campaign.

Bad for farmers, bad for people

Land reform in Zimbabwe has failed to reduce rural poverty. Ownership is no longer dominated by white farmers but by an elite group of ZANU-PF loyalists, reflecting the "Zanuisation" of land ownership. Under Fast Track reforms, 178 well-connected blacks received farms larger than 150,000 hectares and 50 black landowners secured more than one farm.[7] The liberation-war slogan of "one man, one farm" is a distant memory.

The new commercial farmers are mainly black, but labour relations remain largely unchanged. This contrasts with the experience of land reform in East Asia, where class differentiation has been a major impetus for redistribution.

Fast Track land reform exacerbated the marginalisation of women in Zimbabwe, although the proportion of female beneficiaries varied by region. The percentage of medium-sized farms (Model A2) allocated to women were as follows: Midlands (5%), Masvingo (8%), Mashonaland Central (13%), Mashonaland West (11%), Matebeleland North (17%) and Manicaland (9%).[8]

The disruption caused a fall in agricultural production which is greater than the impact of drought alone. Maize production in the large-scale commercial farming sector fell to 80,000 tonnes in 2003, from 648,000 tonnes in 1999.[9] Zimbabwe's national requirement of maize is 480,000 tonnes. The 2007 harvest was less than 86,000 tonnes – well short of the government's target of 375,000 tonnes.

By causing production of staple crops to drop, land reform has alarming implications for food security. The United Nations food agency appealed for US$118m in expanded food aid for Zimbabwe and pledged to assist about 3.3 million starving citizens in August 2007.[10] The regime has blamed sanctions for derailing the fruits of Fast Track land reform, although it was the violent method of land reform that provided the justification for sanctions.

An independent land and agrarian commission

Even though "ownership" has been deracialised, the new allocation of land is highly undemocratic. A new elite of black landlords control large holdings of prime farmland. The priority must be to create conditions for an egalitarian, and de-Zanuised, system of ownership that addresses the plight of the dispossessed.

The current redistribution outcome can be reversed. Failure to reverse a dispensation which vests the best land in the hands of a ZANU-PF elite, would create fertile ground for further social and political unrest. New forms of land tenure under multiple ownership need to be developed for the redistribution of large holdings, under the auspices of an independent land and agrarian commission.

The new commission would audit state and private land to establish who got what, when and how during *jambanja* (a term used to describe the violent, chaotic and disorderly land occupations). The audit would establish the extent of unused and under-utilised land, and the number of individuals owning more than one farm. Once an audit is completed, I propose that the new commission adopt the following priorities:

- Redistribution: under-utilised or unused state land should be further redistributed to the marginalised farm workers, women, politically excluded groups, rural poor and competent farmers; a policy of "one household, one farm" could replace the slogan "one man, one farm" .
- Security of tenure: poor households who received land under Fast Track should be supported in formalising their rights to land: many have failed to do so, in part from fear of incurring liabilities under any subsequent reversal of the policy. The same right of tenure can be extended to those members of the ZANU-PF political elite who qualify under a new policy of one household, one farm.
- Reversing elite capture: excessive land holdings and the possession of multiple farms by a political elite need to be addressed, and the land redistributed.

- Wider agrarian reform: technical support in the form of farming inputs and fair pricing for services should be available to deserving beneficiaries; policy-makers will need to take account of land use and the needs of farmers, in devising new strategies for infrastructural development, reform of parastatals and rural development.

The more things stay the same

Land ownership in Zimbabwe has been deracialised, but agrarian relations reminiscent of the colonial era persist. A black elite, loyal to ZANU-PF, has replaced white elites in the prime farming zones. Women, farm workers, the rural poor and non-ZANU-PF supporters have been largely excluded.

The discourse of a "Just Land" policy, which evolved during the liberation struggle and in the early years of majority rule, has failed. As the National Constitutional Assembly, a broad-based civil society group, has argued: "Can we therefore say the struggle is over when the system has not changed?" The struggle for land is not yet over.

Phillan Zamchiya *is former president of the Zimbabwean National Union of Students and a graduate student in the land and agrarian studies department of the University of the Western Cape.*

No quick fix

Zimbabwe has the resources and potential for economic revival, but it will need international help and access to credit. **Eric Bloch**, *independent advisor to the Reserve Bank of Zimbabwe, sets out his priorities.*

The economy is in disarray and shrinking at a rapid pace. Official inflation figures are the highest in the world and the real rate undoubtedly higher. Agricultural output, the foundation of our economy, is less than 20% of levels of 10 years ago.

An estimated 84% of the population subsists below the Poverty Datum Line. Worse, it is calculated that an horrendous 57% of Zimbabweans survive on incomes below the Food Datum Line. More starkly, this means that more than half the population is malnourished and facing ill-health or early death.

As export earnings have slumped, a massive shortage of foreign exchange has arisen in the absence of significant foreign investment, lines of credit and much developmental aid. Many essential commodities are scarce, including antiretroviral drugs for people with AIDS, basic medications, fuel, electricity, industrial and agricultural inputs, and much else. The shortages have fuelled a virile black market in foreign currency, and any other scarce commodities, thereby driving inflation still higher.

Nevertheless, an economic transformation is readily possible.

Zimbabwe has fertile land, but that land must be used productively. Beneath that land lies vast wealth: uranium, platinum, gold, diamonds, nickel, coal, methane gas, and more. Very little of it has been extracted. The landscape is blessed with spectacular tourist attractions – Victoria Falls, Great Zimbabwe Ruins, Matopos Hills, Lake Kariba Nyanga, Bvumba mountains – and much wild life.

Despite the economic morass, Zimbabwe has the second most developed industrial infrastructure in southern Africa, ideally located to supply a regional free trade area with a population of 326 million. Most of all, it has 11.4 million people, of whom 11.3 million are among the most hard-working, aspirational people on earth. Their lives are being destroyed by 100,000 others.

An economic metamorphosis requires diverse, consistent and committed actions. It is illusory to believe that Zimbabwe can "go it alone". Recovery depends on eight key actions to repair international relations:

- Absolute respect for international norms of human rights.
- A free and independent judiciary to uphold the rule of law.
- Unequivocal observance of, and regard for, property rights.
- Acceptance of constructive criticisms from the international community
- An end to the meaningless, non-yielding "Look East" policy, in favour of a reciprocally beneficial "Look North, South, East and West" policy.
- Reform of the ill-conceived and grossly mismanaged land reform programme: land reform is needed, but it has to be just and equitable; the outcome should enhance agricultural production, instead of destroying it.
- Respect for bilateral investment protection agreements to encourage and facilitate the return of white farmers, while increasing the number of black farmers; recipients of land should be selected on merit, not nepotism.
- Substantial devaluation of the currency pending allowing it to float at an early future date: this will reduce the scarcity of foreign exchange, while stimulating enhanced fiscal inflows.

Other distortions need to be removed as part of a broader scheme of economic deregulation. These include an absence of "real" interest rates, and a plethora of unrealistic state subsidies which are often abused.

Hand in hand with these actions, the government must create a genuinely welcoming investment environment by developing infrastructure. Parastatals should be targeted for privatisation. Public spending must be reined in, reducing the excessive number of ministries, embassies, consulates and missions around the world, and never-ending global travels by the political elite.

There is no quick fix but if these and other actions are positively pursued, they will succeed. The country can, in time, have a dynamic and vigorous economy.

Extracted from an article first published in the *Mail & Guardian* newspaper, May 4th 2007, and edited for clarity.

"We are printing money to build roads and dams"

The influence of **Gideon Gono**, *governor of the Reserve Bank, has grown since foreign creditors cut balance of payments support in 1998. He tells* **Baffour Ankomah** *about hyperinflation, increased dependence on South Africa, and his own role in planning and policy.*[1]

GG: Economies, the world over, are like human beings. They go through ups and downs. Contemporary history is full of economies that have gone through worse challenges than ours, where they have gone through inflation levels that could not fit into a 16-digit calculator.

Germany went through inflation levels that were reaching trillions. Argentina went through inflation levels that were above 5,000%. They had a budget deficit of over 80%. I could give you more examples. Brazil, for instance, Israel and many other countries went through the same bad patches and implemented programmes that brought inflation down from 6,000% to single digits in short spaces of time. If they could do it, who says we can't? We are busy laying the foundations for a serious deceleration programme.

What makes our economy and our inflation unique is that our challenges are multi-dimensional. Ours are predominantly political – political in the sense that they have their roots in the differences that Zimbabwe has had with its former colonial master, the UK, who, together with other allies, have imposed economic and political sanctions on us. As a result, we have not had balance of payments support since 1998. You show me a country that has been so vilified and survived.

We also suffered from exogenous factors such as drought. This economy is agro-based and the fortunes, or misfortunes, in agriculture play a significant role in our performance. In other words, there is a positive correlation between the drought and inflation. If you study the pattern of our droughts, every 10 years up to 2002 we have had droughts.

Then because of the changing weather patterns, we've now been having more frequent droughts; 2003, 2004 and 2006 into 2007. If you combine the drought and the lack of balance of payments support and international sanctions, you have got the makings of a difficult economic environment.

How are you going to tame inflation if it's driven by causes you can't control?
We are predicting all recovery strategies on agricultural recovery. Having gone through sometimes destructive stages of land reform – the emotive periods – we are now focusing on making the land productive. We have embarked on a serious irrigation programme which the central bank is financing.

Ordinarily, this infrastructure should be financed by soft loans from development institutions like the World Bank and the others, but we have had to print money. We are printing money to build dams and buy irrigation equipment. It means that where we used the land once a year, we are now going to be using the same land three times a year for cropping. Simple arithmetic tells you we will regain our breadbasket status of yesteryear.

Your critics have been saying that you are printing too much money.
These are armchair critics. Only the bullfighter knows exactly what goes on in the ring. It's easy to criticise, but what alternatives do they proffer in an environment where we can't get the traditional balance of payments support, the traditional development support?

If you look at the impact of sanctions on this economy, you will then see how the drying up of resources has affected us. The United States had to print money to finance some of the infrastructure that the current generation are proud to have. I'm just being practical and pragmatic: what others would call economics of adaptation and survival – that's what we are doing.

You have said that your role is unique in Africa.
Yes, there is no other comparison. We are guided by conviction and not convention, and where convention meets conviction, well and good. Those who wrote the economic texts of yesteryear – Keynes and others – were not living in an environment where the IMF and the World Bank existed. None of them lived in an era where a revolutionary land reform programme was going on under a revolutionary government. They did not live in an era where the man spearheading that revolution was called Robert Gabriel Mugabe.

But isn't this the role of the finance minister?
Land reform is a fundamental policy of the government, just like infrastructure development. In an environment where the economy is not flourishing the only line of defence, and I must say the last line of defence, is the power within ourselves to print money.

We don't need foreign exchange to build roads and dams. We need local currency. So we print the money here to finance infrastructure development, because infrastructure is not inflationary. We are saying we shall suffer the burden of infrastructural development. Inflation will go up, yes; but the real value is understood in the pain of attainment. Easy come, easy go.

Zimbabwe has more dams than any other country in Africa, and yet your agriculture is still dependant on rainfall.
It's not about just keeping the water. It has purpose when it is taken where it is needed most. The economic model of the past has created a few white elephants. All we are doing now is completing the process, and soon we will be out of the woods.

Can you confirm that the current programme of mechanisation, buying tractors and other equipment for farmers, has also benefited members of the opposition MDC?
Let me first position the mechanisation programme in the economic turnaround policy of the country and land reform. With agriculture, the greatest weakness in the chain was identified as mechanisation. In Brazil and other successful agricultural countries, you will find that mechanisation was a key factor. During our land reform programme, a great deal of equipment found its way across our borders and we needed to replace it.

You mean the white farmers took it away?
That's correct. Last year alone, we lost tremendous amounts of wheat to early rains. It was so painful to see a farmer watching helplessly as the wheat was destroyed. Hence, we brought in state-of-the-art combine harvesters that will do 140 hectares per day, and we have distributed them across the country.

The task of feeding the nation cannot be left to one political party, or one village or institution or a group of people. We are an apolitical central bank that supports the government. So yes, it's not just the MDC, members of other political parties also received tractors and other equipment.

Let's turn to the hyperinflation caused by the inordinate escalation of prices.
The wave of price increases – the madness, the selfishness, and the greed – was something that no sane government would allow to go unchecked. It was a direct attack on the core function of the central bank. So any efforts to control that madness are things that this bank and governor welcome.

Where we differed with the Price Stabilisation Taskforce was the one-sided nature of addressing the demand side of the equation. I called for, and we continue to call for, a holistic approach to the exercise – one that recognises that there has to be production and, therefore, the supply side has to be taken care of by ensuring that it is not disrupted. When a nation is going through difficulties, the last thing we need is for people to lose their heads. All we are saying is that two wrongs don't make a right.

We hear that business is now working behind the scenes with the government.
Yes. The whole essence of trying to come up with a Social Contract – which was mooted by this bank in January 2007 and which we worked on as advisors for 120 days – was exactly to achieve a harmonious working environment between government and business. We had indicated in January that if we didn't take steps to deal with this situation, we would find ourselves in an environment we had never experienced before.

It does not matter how brutal the fight has been, ultimately there is no substitute for government, business and labour going back to the Social Contract. President Mugabe has been consistent on this issue and what he said at the national shrine, the Heroes Acre, recently, is consistent with what he said in his State of the Nation address on December 2nd 2003: "We are all witnesses to the futility of trying to turn around our economy in an environment of pointless conflict. We are all Zimbabweans and must work to correct and amend whatever shortcomings as a family." He has even said that to his political contenders in the MDC: "Let's talk about our differences like brothers," he told them.

Given what has happened to Zimbabwe in recent years, do you still have faith in the international financial system?

Probably I should say we now have greater faith in ourselves than outside ourselves. We will welcome support from whatever quarter, but that support should be predicated on actions that we take voluntarily. We have been very disappointed by the politicisation of institutions that are supposed to be apolitical.

Is there any point, then, in Zimbabwe still being a member of the IMF?

Yes, there is a point. There is a need for us to reform these institutions. We will continue to remain a member, but working for its transformation.

There are people who are afraid of China, but President Mugabe said that China is now Zimbabwe's biggest cooperation partner in the East.

What have you got to fear from those that have proven themselves in terms of sincerity and ability to transform their own situation? China went through an economic reform programme that has transformed that country. So, yes, those with wayward behaviour, who don't want to work hard, those who want to play the parallel market and those who are ill-disposed to discipline, have everything to fear when the Chinese and our "Look East" partners come.

How much does the economic growth rate of South Africa depend on doing business with Zimbabwe?

Well, the South African economy is a huge one. You are looking at their population of over 56m versus ours of about 12m; a GDP that is about 15 times the size of ours. In their own scheme of things, we may not be that important.

But our total global import bill from 1998 to 2006 has been averaging US$2bn a year. Of that, over 50% – sometimes 55% as it happened last year – has been coming from South Africa. This economy has been operating as a cash economy for seven years with no lines of credit. What that means is that in 2005, for instance, we paid out US$1.17bn, or 53.4%, of our total import bill in cash for importing goods from South Africa. In 1998, that figure was 34%.

Our exports to South Africa have also been growing. But this time on extended credit terms. Last year, out of US$1.73bn global exports 39%, or US$684m, went to South Africa. In other words, Zimbabwean firms are giving South Africans credit terms even though they would not extend credit to us.

Why is that encouraged?
This is it – the international terms of trade.

Tell me, why should any investor look at Zimbabwe in its current state?
This is a multi-dimensional economy, a diversified economy, the second largest and most prosperous economy in sub-Saharan Africa. The literacy levels are the highest in Africa at 94%. This is an economy that is providing the rest of the world with manpower, including in the UK. Never mind what kind of jobs these are, it is the resilience, honesty and integrity of Zimbabweans as born and bred by the education system under this government. Others call it brain drain, but we would call it an export of professionalism to the rest of the world.

With South Africa we have 80% of the world's platinum deposits. We have the largest reserves of methane gas in sub-Saharan Africa, according to US statistics. We have over 40 different minerals beneath our soil. Show me any other country in Africa, apart from South Africa, with the depth and breadth of financial services and infrastructure that we have here.

I'm not saying every part of our infrastructure is working. There are some local authorities and parastatals that need revamping. So given the choice of who to befriend – one who has been in battle, who has been tried and tested – I don't think there is any doubt as to whose credentials you will pick.

For this economy to stabilise, there has to be a steady supply of fuel.
Yes, I agree. This economy imports 70% of manufacturing raw materials and we need fuel. When they say oil drives the wheels of industry and commerce, it is true. We need a sustained supply of fuel and electricity, and an injection of capital to take advantage of all the raw materials and minerals beneath our soil. We are a sleeping giant.

Let's talk properly now about the IMF. I want you to talk from the bottom of your heart.
From the fount of my heart, we could have been handled more fairly. There is no other country in recorded history that has received such bad treatment as Zimbabwe at the hands of the IMF. I can speak with authority because I was in the trenches and I saw what was happening there.

We trusted them, we gave them information, we opened our hearts to them, and we opened our strong-rooms for them to gather data. When they went back, they abused that access. It would not happen here. We feel violated.

The worst part was the experience of the Zimbabwean delegation to the IMF Executive Board meeting on March 8th 2006, when rules were changed midstream during the Board meeting. It was tragic, and it will remain tragic in the history books of the IMF. This is why I have said reliance and sustenance have got to come from ourselves and not primarily from outsiders.

I know Zimbabwe is fighting a war even though the other side would not admit it. Well, let me just say Zimbabwe will not die. We'll have bruises here and there, but we will not die. And we will also not tell the whole world our strategies for survival because we have been betrayed before.

Gideon Gono *is governor of the Reserve Bank of Zimbabwe.* **Baffour Ankomah** *is editor of* New African *magazine.*

Neighbourly advice

SADC leaders discussed the priorities for reforming economic policy in Zimbabwe at their summit in Lusaka in August 2007. This excerpt from a text agreed at the summit was published in the ANC newsletter ANC Today.

"The restoration of the country's foreign exchange generating capacity through Balance of Payments support is crucial: however, the most urgent action that is needed to start this process is to establish lines of credit to enable Zimbabwe to import inputs for its productive sectors, particularly for agriculture and foreign currency generating sectors.

"SADC should do all it can to help Zimbabwe address the issue of sanctions, which is not only hurting the economy through failure to get BoP support and lines of credit, but also through reduced markets for its products. Sanctions also damage the image of Zimbabwe, causing a severe blow to her tourist sector.

"Zimbabwe on her part must continue to implement robust policies to reduce the overvaluation of the exchange rate, to reduce the budget deficit and to control the growth of domestic credit and money supply which fuel inflation, and to reduce price distortions in the economy. Equally important is the need to avoid frequent changes in policy initiatives, which have caused uncertainties and led to the view that the policy environment is unpredictable."

Did the farmers deserve it?

White liberals in the former Rhodesia took a dim view of the commercial farmers,
recalls **Diana Mitchell**. *Many anticipated the pact between farmers and nationalists*
would sour, but a terrible price has been exacted for the self-interested myopia of
landowners.

The once fertile fields, fat cattle and giant tobacco barns – with their bountiful harvest
of hard currency – are now history. Robert Mugabe's revenge has been wreaked upon
Zimbabwe's white commercial farmers – and Africans watched, often with approval,
as an African repossessed African land.

That was the preferred excuse in sub-Saharan Africa, but it ignored the truth. Mugabe
made his move when white farmers openly supported a political opposition. The
Movement for Democratic Change – led by a relatively young, former official of the
Zimbabwe Congress of Trade Unions – was growing in popularity. Mugabe's ZANU-
PF was not.

Before 2000, Zimbabwe was a demi-paradise, if you owned thousands of acres of
prime, agricultural land and had the know-how to exploit it. Commercial farming
was the bedrock of the nation's prosperity for about three decades before the white
settler government was removed from power in 1980, and for another two decades
since the birth of Zimbabwe as a new African independent nation.

The benefits of this economic legacy are more evident now that thousands of white
farmers have been evicted: the few hundred who remain are there only at the mercy
of the government. The question still needs to be asked, however: did the country's
white farmers deserve their fate?

To this question, I submit a qualified "yes". A part of this tragedy has its roots in the
arrogance, or ignorance, of the majority of privileged Rhodesian whites. Commercial
farmers voted slavishly for Ian Douglas Smith, whose Rhodesian Front party
promised that "Smithy" would keep things good for them.

As it turned out, commercial farmers have been driven off the land, dispossessed,
and some even killed. Their workers find themselves homeless and suffering. Land-

hungry peasants have become instruments of a gigantic kleptocracy, falsely promised fat rewards of prime land and financial help. Many had, themselves, fought for repossession of their lands in the guerrilla war.

A hunger for land

I became involved with Rhodesia's white liberal opposition in the last years of Smithy's minority government. Together with our few black supporters, we actively opposed his shortsighted politics. We insisted that land hunger was real, and that this, together with racial segregation, would be the country's undoing.

We beat our opposition drum to little effect. With the staunch backing of "Royal Game", as the white farmers were then known, Smith's Rhodesian Front government imprisoned and restricted black political leaders: Ndabaningi Sithole, Joshua Nkomo, Robert Mugabe and hundreds of others. The farmers were scornful of our warnings.

International pressure eventually secured the release of the imprisoned nationalists, but Smithy's Rhodesian Front opted too late for an "internal settlement" with moderate black leadership. Scores of lives were sacrificed in a fruitless attempt to counter a guerrilla war, led by militant black nationalists and armed by "friends" in the communist bloc of the cold war era.

A largely collaborative media ensured that Smithy's followers – the enfranchised few – were willfully blinkered from reality. The official opposition, a despised minority within a minority, were members of our multi-racial Centre Party. We were branded traitors and "communist fellow travellers". The Rhodesian Front accused us of letting the side down in their campaign to preserve "Christian western civilisation".

For all their rhetoric, a conventional white-led military machine, often gung-ho in its activities and reliant on black Rhodesian troops, could not defeat the guerrilla insurrection crossing the borders from newly independent Mozambique and other "frontline" states. Smithy's only ally, the apartheid government in South Africa, wisely threw in the towel as its own day of reckoning approached.

From reconciliation to land grab

White farmers clung tenaciously and bravely to their farms, in the front line of guerrilla attacks. Their refusal to abandon a fertile agricultural economy was acknowledged when Mugabe's government initially appointed Dennis Norman, a white farmer, as minister of agriculture. His name was recommended to the ZANU-PF leadership by our Centre Party's president, Pat Bashford, a Karoi farmer.

These farmers who stayed after independence were fooled by Mugabe's promises of reconciliation. But by the time the land grab was seriously underway in 2000, 75% of these white farms had already changed hands. Commercial farmers bought and sold them with the consent of Mugabe's government. Hence the answer to my question about the blameworthiness of commercial farmers – a qualified "yes". They did not deserve wholesale eviction.

Farmers, and ultimately all Zimbabweans, have paid a terrible price for a collective failure to redress the century-long resentment felt by the landless black majority. They failed to recognise that the end of the war of liberation was not the end of land hunger. They were arrogant, and many are still racist.

Just as Mugabe's land appropriations have been wrong, white farmers have paid a terrible price for the errors of their own leadership. Instead of pro-active land-sharing policies, Smith's minority government preferred a unilateral declaration of independence which led Rhodesia into an un-winnable war against its own majority black inhabitants.

In May 2002, *New African* magazine published a 17-page interview with Robert Mugabe by Baffour Ankomah. Zimbabwe's president boasted that in 1979, at the Lancaster House talks in London, western negotiators seeking an end to Zimbabwe's liberation war offered to pay ample compensation for the repossession of white-owned land. Mugabe did not explain what became of this offer, or whether – in his role as Zimbabwe's pre-eminent black nationalist – it was Mugabe himself who chose to ignore it.

Diana Mitchell *was the press and publicity executive officer for the multi-racial Centre Party and its successor, the National Unifying Force, August 1968 – 1984. She is the author of a series of three books of African nationalist biographies.*

Kith and kin

The serial failure of agreements to redistribute land scuppered hopes of a peaceful settlement in Zimbabwe, writes **Thabo Mbeki** *in his online Letter from the President. A mere £9m might have averted a crisis which has simmered since the 19th century.*

The current Zimbabwe crisis started in 1965 when the then British Labour Government, under prime minister Harold Wilson, refused to suppress the rebellion against the British Crown led by Ian Smith. This was because the British Government felt that it could not act against its white "kith and kin", in favour of the African majority.

At the constitutional negotiations in 1979, the British Conservative government insisted that the property and other rights and privileges of this "kith and kin" had to be protected. It therefore ensured that Zimbabwe's independence constitution had entrenched clauses, valid for ten years, which, among other things, protected the property rights of the white settler colonial "kith and kin", including the landowners.

The large sums of money promised by both the British and US governments to enable the new government to buy land for African settlement never materialised. The land dispossession carried out by the settler colonial "kith and kin" through the barrel of the gun had to be sustained, despite the fact that even in 1979, the British government recognised the fact that land was at the core of the conflict in Zimbabwe.

In 1998 we intervened to help mediate the growing tension between Zimbabwe and the UK on the land question. This, and other factors, led to the international conference on the land question held in Zimbabwe that year.

At that conference, the international community, including the UK, the UN, and the EU, agreed to help finance the programme of land redistribution that had been an essential part of the negotiated settlement of 1979 – a settlement which, in return for introducing majority rule, guaranteed the privileges of the white settler colonial "kith and kin". Nothing came of these commitments.

Later, the British government could not find a mere £9 million to buy 118 farms, whose purchase had been agreed at the international conference. These would have been used to resettle the war veterans who had begun to occupy farms owned by the white "kith and kin", continuing a struggle for the return of the land to the indigenous majority, which had started at the end of the 19th century.

Again we intervened to help solve the Zimbabwe land question. We managed to get pledges from various countries, other than the UK, to provide this £9 million. Having handed this matter over to the UN, it collapsed in the intricacies of the UN bureaucracy. Though there were willing sellers and willing buyers, and the necessary funds, the 118 farms were not bought.

With everything having failed to restore the land to its original owners in a peaceful manner, a forcible process of land redistribution perhaps became inevitable. Though we were conscious of the frustration that had built up in Zimbabwe, we urged the government of Zimbabwe, both privately and publicly, to act against the forcible seizure of white farms and other violence in the country. On one of these occasions, at Victoria Falls and in the presence of President Mugabe, I told the world press that, together with Presidents Nujoma and Chissano, we had raised this matter with President Mugabe.

For the record, we must mention that our national broadcaster did not record my comments on this matter. The SABC television team that covered this press conference later explained that at that point it did not have the necessary cassette to record these comments.

Extracted from *ANC Today*, Volume 3, No. 49, 12- 18 December 2003, and edited for clarity.

Zimbabwe's golden leaf

Much of the tobacco industry, Zimbabwe's main source of foreign exchange, has been destroyed by chaotic land resettlement and economic upheaval. This is a severe blow to a crop which was the bedrock of the colonial economy – but it is not fatal. Tobacco will again become important in any recovery strategy, writes **Aoiffe O'Brien**.

The collapse of large-scale commercial farming has dealt a severe blow to Zimbabwe's principal generator of foreign exchange. In 2001, tobacco exports brought US$600m in foreign earnings to Zimbabwe. By 2007, tobacco revenues had fallen to just over US$100m.

In the long-term, the reduction in smoking in industrialised nations implies that tobacco may remain a shrinking market. Other industries, notably mining and natural resources, have the potential to become more important to Zimbabwe's economy. But the agronomic conditions which favoured tobacco in Zimbabwe are not fundamentally changed, and its crop has been prized by international buyers. With concerted effort, tobacco production can recover.

Tobacco farming began in Zimbabwe at the end of the 19th century, quickly becoming an incentive for white settlement. It assumed priority in both colonial agricultural policy and the British South Africa Company. Its profitability earned it the nickname of "the golden leaf" – a reference to the crop's value, not its colour.

By 1980, with 41% of Africa's total crop, Zimbabwe was well established as the continent's leading producer.[1] This dominance was sustained during the first two decades of independence, while tobacco remained the preserve of large-scale, mostly white-owned commercial farms. In the 1990s, just over 81,000 hectares were given to growing tobacco.[2]

Besides foreign exchange, tobacco earnings generated healthy tax revenues for the government of Zimbabwe and fostered valuable secondary markets for inputs such as fertiliser and farm equipment. Industry figures for the 1990s suggest that 28 per cent of a total of 153,404 jobs generated by tobacco were in secondary industries.[3]

After the farm seizures

Tobacco has been the hardest hit of all agricultural sectors since 2000, falling by 60% in the five years to 2005. This compares with an across-the-board fall of 40% spanning all agricultural output for the same period. The Zimbabwe Tobacco Association estimates that 45,000 hectares of tobacco cultivation have been lost in the wake of the chaotic land seizures which began in 1999.[4]

Land reforms have transferred fertile land to people who largely lacked the know-how or the resources to farm tobacco. The selection of farms for resettlement was controlled by committees from the ruling ZANU-PF party, with much of the confiscated land handed to party officials and "war veterans". The seizures caused damage to the infrastructure developed and maintained by commercial farmers, including extensive irrigation systems.

Among many examples, in 2002, Francis Nhema, minister for environment and tourism, assumed control of an 800 hectare farm seized by war veterans. Output slumped to about 20 hectares of maize, from almost 88 hectares of maize and 80 hectares of tobacco, on a farm which previously employed around 250 permanent workers and a further 250 seasonal workers.[5]

Wider economic collapse has exacerbated farmers' problems. Scarcity of fuel and foreign exchange drastically reduced the scope and incentives for tobacco farming. Farmers are able to source imported agricultural inputs on the parallel market, but are mostly constrained by the official rate when converting their dollar-denominated sales into local currency.

In January 2007, the government set the proportion of foreign currency earnings which tobacco farmers can hold at 15%. By law, the lion's share of the proceeds from the tobacco crop must be converted to Zimbabwean dollars at the official exchange rate: this allows the Reserve Bank to capture a share of the profits.

Obstacles to recovery

Next to the generalised problems of political economy, there are three main barriers to recovery in Zimbabwe's tobacco sector:

• First, the legal basis of land ownership is in disarray, while key skills have been lost through emigration. New occupiers of confiscated land have been reluctant to claim legally recognised formal title, for fear of incurring potential liabilities in any subsequent reorganisation of land. Their shaky legal status prevents access to credit and discourages investment in new infrastructure and production.

- Second, the market for Zimbabwean tobacco has been seized by rival producers. Manufacturers of blended cigarettes have found substitutes for the Zimbabwean crop, chiefly from Brazil, but also from other parts of South America and Africa. This has raised fears that demand for Zimbabwean tobacco is unlikely to recover.
- Third, the industry is in long-term decline. Global demand for tobacco has weakened with the reduction in smoking in the largest traditional markets of North America and Europe. Health risks, smoking bans and increased regulation weigh on the long-term prospects for tobacco.

These concerns reflect serious threats to Zimbabwe's tobacco industry, but they are not grounds for despair. An agricultural recovery is viable, but requires a recognised system of land tenure, the provision of adequate support services, rebuilding of irrigation systems and a carefully designed subsidy – at least in the short term – for essential farm inputs.

A reformed, stable mechanism to allocate property rights would encourage consensus among the key political actors and confidence in the agricultural sector. Despite an exodus of skills in the wake of the farm seizures, a significant (if unknowable) proportion of farmers could return.

Prevailing agronomic conditions in Zimbabwe favour tobacco. The crop grows well in sandy soil with low water-holding capacity and tolerates extreme weather conditions. Historically, the Zimbabwean crop has been of a higher quality than the same varieties produced elsewhere.

Cigarette manufacturers maintain that demand for their product is robust. Worldwide, the prevalence of smoking among women is much lower than among men. Among smokers, consumption in developing countries remains much lower than in industrialised nations. Even small increases in smoking among women and in developing countries would significantly raise demand for tobacco.

In summary, the market for Zimbabwean tobacco is not lost. While cigarette manufacturers have found substitutes for Zimbabwean tobacco, it has proved relatively difficult to match its quality. Farmers who moved to Mozambique after the land seizures, for example, have been frustrated by inferior conditions resulting in lower quality crops. Tobacco is more profitable than other agricultural crops, and probably more labour-intensive. British American Tobacco, one of the world's largest cigarette manufacturers, claims that "tobacco creates more employment per hectare of cultivated land than any other crop in the world."[6]

If not tobacco...
Few other crops can bear the expense, or time, of long distance transport. Alternative crops should take priority only if they combine:
• High profitability per hectare.
• Stable markets.
• Adaptability to local conditions.
• Labour-intensive production.

By these criteria, horticulture is the best alternative prospect for land previously dedicated to tobacco. In the late 1990s, vegetable and rose exports performed well. In 2000, export earnings from these crops reached US$124.9m.[7] Horticultural crops have a stable market and create at least as many jobs per hectare as tobacco. However, tobacco farmers benefit from long experience of the export market. Established quality control procedures and auctions mean tobacco benefits from a marketing infrastructure that is not yet available in horticulture.

Whether farmers decide to grow roses or tobacco, the cost of setting up, or repairing, the necessary infrastructure will be high. Horticulture has the advantage in this sense, as many international lenders and donor organisations are reluctant to support tobacco production. Longer term, the environmental costs of transporting horticultural products may affect the viability of rose exports from Africa. These concerns have been disputed by some environmentalists, however, who point to a greater "greenhouse effect" of farming roses in heated hothouses in Europe.

Beyond agriculture
Like most of sub-Saharan Africa, Zimbabwe remains a largely agricultural economy and – over the long-term – a victim of the downward trend in global commodity prices. Dependence on a few key commodities has hit African producers hardest because,

unlike many of their Asian peers, falling prices have not been offset by gains in productivity. But recent years have brought firmer prices for certain key African commodities, often bolstered by strong demand from China. This augurs well for Africa, including Zimbabwe, but should not obscure the need, in any recovery plan, for new emphasis on improving productivity.

> *"Recent years have brought firmer prices for certain key African commodities, often bolstered by strong demand from China. This should not obscure the need to improve productivity."*

Diversification beyond traditional exports remains vital. Mining has great potential in Zimbabwe, given the variety of its metal and mineral resources. In a robust macro-environment, abundant natural resources would become a magnet for prospective mining companies, buoyed by the continent-wide mining boom. Service industries stand to benefit from a well-educated population, including a high proportion of English speakers. Tourism, devastated by recent upheaval, can recover under stable political conditions. Information and communications technology is poised for exponential growth if the economy rebounds. In 2005, the proportion of cellular phone subscribers was only 54 people in every 1,000. Internet access reached only 77 in every 1,000.[8]

Some doughty foreign investors are waiting in the wings. In 2007, Lonrho – the rump of the resuscitated mining and hotels group headed by the late "Tiny" Rowland – set up a targeted investment fund for Zimbabwe, LonZim. Emma Priestley, executive director at Lonrho, said investors were ready to believe that Zimbabwe has both the human and natural resources capital to support a variety of business activities. She pointed out that despite the current crisis, innovative initiatives, such as ostrich and crocodile farming for high value textiles, are succeeding.[9]

A new role for donors
Pessimists have argued that Zimbabwe has passed a point of no return, beyond which only massive outside assistance can bring recovery.

Donors have hinted, routinely, that more funding would be made available to Zimbabwe in the wake of political reform. They are largely reluctant to reveal their plans for Zimbabwe, although several agencies – including Britain's Foreign and Commonwealth Office and government organisations from the US and Europe – have discussed a preliminary strategy at meetings in London and Amsterdam.[10]

External funding will be critical to manage Zimbabwe's crippling foreign debt. Donors may also take a role in rebuilding state institutions. More important in the short term is the need for new incentives to restore, and improve, agricultural productivity. Subsidies for seeds, fertiliser and irrigation are a logical first step.

Zimbabwe's arable land, mineral resources, good infrastructure and educated population are inherent competitive advantages in a region where most governments are committed to an ambitious programme of economic integration. With the exception of South Africa, Zimbabwe's neighbour and largest trading partner, no other country is better positioned to exploit this trend.

Aoiffe O'Brien *is a researcher at Africa Research Institute.*

Beware foreign aid

Zimbabwe will need donor funds to kickstart a recovery, writes **Beacon Mbiba**, *but foreign funds come with strings attached. Zimbabweans have learned from experience to be wary of donor priorities.*

The promise of aid is one of the standard instruments used by powerful western nations to bring feuding groups to the negotiating table. The Americans and the British, among others, promised aid for land reform and reconstruction as a carrot to win the consent of liberation war leaders to the new Zimbabwean constitution brokered at Lancaster House, London, in 1979.

More recently key western development initiatives, including Tony Blair's Commission for Africa in 2004, have recommended the doubling of aid to sub-Saharan Africa. Total spending by the G8 nations on development funding for Africa is scheduled to double by 2010, increasing by an extra US$48bn a year.

In Zimbabwe, much more money could be made available by donors. The British government is understood to be prepared to "reach out", and "ready to significantly step up" aid to Zimbabwe if the political stalemate can be resolved. The implication is that donor funds are an incentive for a "pragmatic faction" in Africa to remove Mugabe, form a new government, stabilise the economy and restore democracy.

We do not need promises of aid to make these things happen.

Aid is damaging to a developing nation. It distorts our thinking, our priorities and policies, as we have seen in the past with the disputes over land. We need to resolve our political problems and chart a future without the distortions of donor promises, priorities and assistance. Transparent, pro-poor, sustainable land reform can be done without aid from Britain.

When we do accept aid, we have to confront the question of how to use it and how to reduce our dependence in the future.

Donors give aid for moral reasons – they want to help. But there is also an element of self-interest that is damaging to recipients of aid. Thus donor policies are contradictory.

Over the past sixty years, US development policy in Africa frustrated the progress of democracy and popular liberation movements in southern Africa. During the Cold War, the criteria for allocating aid included real or perceived alignment with the Soviet Union. Today, post 9/11, international relations are determined by fears for security, markets and oil.

The UN Millennium Project report, published in 2005, gives a damning verdict on aid. The report states that it is often:
- Highly unpredictable (as we saw with British aid for land reform in Zimbabwe)
- Targeted at technical assistance (where the bulk of the money goes back to the donor country).
- Emergency aid rather than investment in long-term capacity and institutional support.
- Tied to contractors from donor countries.
- Driven by separate donor objectives rather than coordinated support to national plans of the recipient country.

A recurrent feature of aid – and a factor in these problems – is that donor funds are often poorly administered. They act to extend the geopolitical interests and agendas of donor nations. Often, more money is spent on administration than on relieving poverty.

Zimbabweans cannot make the promise of aid a basis on which to develop a process for resolving our immediate crisis. We know that pledges may never materialise. If they do, they will distort our national processes, entrench aid dependency and make us vulnerable to the political preferences of the donors.

Zimbabwe has abundant mineral, agricultural and natural resources. Without corruption and misallocation of scarce resources, these sectors can be brought back at least to their peak of the 1980s. We are told that as many as four million Zimbabweans are working abroad, in southern Africa and as far afield as Canada, Israel, New Zealand and the United States; and, of course, in "Harare North" – a.k.a. Great Britain. Among them are scientists, administrators, professionals and entrepreneurs. They will be the first line of investors in Zimbabwe – if conditions are right.

So, the serious national debate must start now. We may need to accept donor funds in the short term because we do not have financial resources to kickstart a recovery. What do we have to do? What resources do we have? Whose aid should we accept? How do we make sure such aid is effective?

Agriculture

Agriculture is the first of two priorities for development. Zimbabwe has agricultural experience and expertise, both within and beyond its borders. We must draw on this resource to map a strategy for our national agricultural recovery.

Smallholder farmers need to be empowered to produce for the commercial market and to achieve food security. Investment is required in rural infrastructure, including in the reconstruction of roads and dams destroyed by cyclones in recent years. It is essential to restore the vitality of the staple crops by improving seed supply. The livestock sector must be restocked. Competitiveness requires the elimination of diseases, such as foot and mouth, in order to regain our export markets.

The private sector can play a key role in boosting agricultural productivity, but public investment will be required in the medium term. Over the past twenty years, donors have been reluctant to fund research institutions and agricultural infrastructure. Aid money can fund the purchase of medicines and rehabilitation of veterinary infrastructure, so that farmers can shoulder the full cost in future. Aid should also support wholesale trading and agro-processing at the local level. These areas are key to employment creation, food security, improvement in rural incomes and poverty alleviation.

Avoiding donor dependence

The second priority for Zimbabwe is to avoid donor dependence. Significant changes to the economy, system of land tenure and demographic structure have occurred since the mid 1990s. These changes have led to some positive as well as negative outcomes for national development. We must start from an assessment of these changes and their impacts. The message to our leaders is that they must not be compromised again.

In the 1980s, Zimbabwe was supported by a variety of donors but avoided becoming donor-dependent. Their funds made up no more than 10% of the country's foreign receipts. Aid supported critical social services and infrastructure projects, and often complimented the government's own resources.

The neo-liberal economic reforms of the 1990s eroded the capacity – or priority – in government to empower the poor. Total aid to Zimbabwe declined as donors shifted their attention and commitment to South Africa (following majority rule), Namibia and Mozambique. With the end of apartheid in South Africa, Zimbabwe's economic and regional significance for donors declined. Simultaneously, donors preferred to point to "a corrupt regime" as their main reason for turning away from Zimbabwe.

The past ten years have seen further decline in development aid from the UK, but a rise in humanitarian assistance. The pattern is similar with other donors including the Dutch and the Scandinavians. In future, effective development partnerships will require emphatic reversals of these trends: from humanitarian assistance to project support such as rehabilitation and maintenance of infrastructure.

Friends of Zimbabwe should support aid which empowers Zimbabweans, for instance in the construction and rehabilitation of roads, dams, service centres and

---

Six months after his election, Mugabe accused Britain of reneging on the deal brokered just over a year before at Lancaster House in London. This report from November 2nd 1980 quotes a figure of US$48m earmarked in British aid to fund the acquisition and development of white-owned farms by blacks, with British officials expecting an equal contribution from the government in Harare.

Farms in Zimbabwe may be confiscated

Mugabe says he lacks the money to pay whites for their land as British support lags

Mount Darwin, Zimbabwe, Nov. 2 (AP) – Prime minister Robert Mugabe says his government may have to seize white-owned farms without paying compensation to the owners.

Mr. Mugabe, speaking at a rally yesterday said his government desperately needed good farmland for resettlement of blacks displaced by the seven-year guerrilla war that brought him to power six months ago.

He said Britain, which ruled Zimbabwe as the colony of Rhodesia, had reneged on pre-independence pledges of money to help his government buy land owned by whites. Mr. Mugabe said British officials have told him that Britain does not have money enough to pay for the land. "And we also say we do not have the money," Mr. Mugabe added.

The British Foreign Office said that the government of prime minister Margaret Thatcher had never made a specific pledge for land reimbursements during the pre-independence talks at Lancaster House in London last year.

'No Figures Bandied About'

"During the Lancaster House conference no figures were bandied about at all," a Foreign Office representative said in London. However, she said the equivalent of $48 million in British aid was due to be used, along with an equal contribution from the Zimbabwe government, for land resettlement projects.

The Foreign Office declined to comment on whether Britain would take action if Mugabe's government confiscated land, which would contravene the constitution agreed on at the talks.

telecommunications. They should avoid a disturbing trend among donor perspectives to treat Africa and Africans as material for experimentation. This trend tends also to exaggerate decline – in Zimbabwe and in Africa generally. Exaggeration reinforces the view that only the West can provide a route to development, setting the stage once again for donors to experiment with any number of new economic programmes, commissions, studies and initiatives.

Zimbabweans and true friends of Zimbabwe should guard against this risk by defending investment in programmes formulated by Zimbabweans.

Dr **Beacon Mbiba** *is senior lecturer and leader in the Planning in Developing Countries and Transition Economies programme at Oxford Brookes University. In 2004-5, he served as an adviser to Tony Blair's Africa Commission.*

Mr. Mugabe previously pledged not to take white land without compensation, and the constitution precludes nationalization of private property without adequate financial compensation.

"No government decision has been taken to change our policy on land compensation," a spokesman for Mr. Mugabe, Godfrey Chanetsa, said today, "but we are appealing for aid to help buy the land we desperately need."

Whites own half of the land
Mr. Mugabe's government has repeatedly said it recognizes the contribution made by the country's 5,500 white farmers, who produce most of the nation's food and earn more than half of its foreign currency. The white farmers own more than half of Zimbabwe's arable land.

Mr. Mugabe's government also has made it a top priority to settle hundreds of thousands of blacks on better land than the crowded, overgrazed land they now inhabit. Britain has pledged $180 million in aid to Zimbabwe during the next three years. Several other western countries, including the United States, have also made pledges.

The sums fall well short of a multibillion-dollar aid package discussed in 1976. Henry A. Kissinger,

who was secretary of state at the time, joined Britain in an abortive attempt to persuade Ian D. Smith's white-minority government to yield power to the black majority.

Lord Soames, governor of Rhodesia during the five months of direct rule by London after the Lancaster House conference and before independence elections, has criticized western governments for not being more generous with aid. In the view of Lord Soames and other critics, generous financial aid would help keep Zimbabwe free of influence from the Eastern bloc.

The Mugabe government established relations today with East Germany, the East German press agency A.D.N. reported.

The Zimbabwe government has had somewhat strained relations with the Soviet-bloc nations, who supported Mugabe's political rival, Joshua Nkomo, during the seven-year guerrilla war against white-minority rule. Mr. Mugabe's guerrillas were backed by China.

The Soviet Union does not have an embassy in Zimbabwe, although Mr. Mugabe recently invited it to establish one.

This article was first published in the *New York Times*, November 3rd 1980.

3. AN AFRICAN DILEMMA

Taking Africa's name in vain

Regional leaders have adopted high standards for Africa's new institutions, reflecting the great moral concerns of their continent's history. But governments have struggled to translate principle into action, writes **Tawanda Mutasah**.

The tooth fairy is harmless folklore, and useful to comfort a child confronted with the loss of a prized milk tooth. But what happens when the leadership of an entire region promises to put money under Robert Mugabe's pillow while he continues to ride roughshod over his economy and people?

At their August 2007 summit in Lusaka, Zambia, heads of state from the Southern African Development Community (SADC) "mandated" their finance ministers to "draw up an economic plan to support Zimbabwe".

It was not made clear why Zimbabwe, which at the height of economic sanctions against Ian Smith's Rhodesia had been the second largest economy in southern Africa, was today in need of support from its neighbours – except by Mugabe. For him, repeating the word "sanctions" serves to disguise all the excesses of a classic lootocracy: the parceling out of land and businesses to the judges, cabinet ministers, senior army officers, intelligence and police operatives whose loyalty Mugabe needs.

Members of this elite club generate stupendous profits from the rent-seeking activities made possible by deliberately self-serving policies. They deal for their own advantage in lines of credit procured by the central bank, and in the productive assets of state industries. Economic collapse has facilitated hedonistic levels of consumption by a small political-military elite, while the poor endeavour to escape hunger by swimming across the Limpopo.

In many ways, the discussion of Zimbabwe at the SADC summit crystallised its translation into a regional and African crisis. The meeting was surrounded by intrigue – sparked by the arrest in Lusaka of Zimbabwean civic leader Tapera Kapuya and the deportation of more than sixty activists ostensibly on the grounds that their "Save Zimbabwe" campaign T-shirts were a threat to peace and security.

A regional prism

It has become increasingly evident that, although primarily a national phenomenon, the Zimbabwe crisis is being played out through a regional prism. To the extent that political problems in Harare can be distilled into a contest for legitimacy, the SADC has framed the context in which bad leadership can be confronted.

The government of South Africa, in particular, has three times provided a new lease of life to Mugabe – by declaring the results of fraudulent and violent elections in June 2000, March 2002 and March 2005 to be legitimate.

For his part, Mugabe has sought to portray the crisis as mainly a dispute about land between Harare and London. Taking southern Africans for undiscerning airheads, Mugabe has used this rhetoric as a curtain behind which to hide gross abuses. These include torture and abductions of mostly black civic and political dissenters; banning and bombing of newspapers and independent radio stations; beatings by police of lawyers, civic and opposition leaders; and eviction from their homes of 700,000 poor Zimbabweans.

When, during his final days in office, outgoing British prime minister Tony Blair visited President Thabo Mbeki in Pretoria, Zimbabwe's state-controlled daily newspaper reported the visit as an humiliation. According to a gloating report in *The Herald*, Blair travelled to Pretoria to enlist support for the opposition in Zimbabwe. Mugabe told party cadres in ZANU-PF that Mbeki "told former British prime minister, Tony Blair, to back off from meddling in the affairs of Zimbabwe as SADC was handling the matter."[1]

In several ways parts of the African continent, particularly Pretoria, have helped to sustain dictatorship in Harare. These include voting at the United Nations Human Rights Council to block discussion on human rights in Zimbabwe; seeking to block the expulsion of Zimbabwe from the Commonwealth; allowing non-payment by parastatal companies for electricity supplied to Zimbabwe; and mitigating the impact on Harare of international sanctions.

At a diplomatic level, discussions of Zimbabwe's problem have used terms so nebulous as to frustrate any meaningful response from African or global meetings. Two sophistries of language have been deployed by Pretoria: that this active solidarity with Mugabe is "quiet diplomacy"; and that Zimbabweans are being left to solve their own problems.

Ring-fencing a crisis

Zimbabweans never had a problem understanding that the Zimbabwean crisis will be solved by Zimbabweans. However, it is also obvious that dictatorship is, for any people, never a domestic matter alone. Zimbabwe trades with other countries and passes its imports, including guns and bullets for domestic repression, through the air, land and sea of other countries.

The government in Harare cites the norms and standards of other countries to claim legal and moral legitimacy. Its dictatorship courts the solidarity of kindred souls outside its borders and seeks at least the tacit approval of other nations for its elections and "democratic" practice. No remedy has ever been devised to end oppression by an armed and violent regime of an unarmed population without external support – not in apartheid South Africa, not in colonial Rhodesia, not anywhere else.

African leaders may claim to wield the "legitimacy" and "tact" to engage Mugabe, but this is not what has happened. Blocking the attempt to censure Zimbabwe for human rights abuses at the United Nations and certifying bad elections as good is not quiet diplomacy. While the sentiment has often been expressed that those who want to be effective in their correction of Harare's human rights misdeeds must beat Mugabe with an African stick and not a Western rod, Zimbabweans have seen no result from African censure.

Not that they love Mugabe, but they love the West less

Mugabe has invested in propaganda aimed at mobilising the continent to the defence of Harare's lootocrats. His government spent an estimated US$1 million on a sponsored supplement in *New African* magazine in a bid to explain away the brutalities of March 11th 2007. This has been accompanied by diversionary national theatrics, such as the church-driven "national vision" process, and poker-faced untruths: a 13-page document issued by the foreign ministry to African embassies claimed that opposition leader Morgan Tsvangirai was "at no time...assaulted while in police custody."

These campaigns have obscured the mechanisms by which a small elite – guns veiled thinly under statutory instruments – can loot businesses, land, agricultural equipment, public service jobs and central bank credit with impunity. Their energies are devoted not to a genuine resolution of crisis, but to keeping Mugabe in power. Insecurity shackles

Mugabe to the presidential chair, while propping up the pretence at a national level of cohesion in the ruling ZANU-PF.

In response, the SADC and the African Union have failed to hold Mugabe accountable to the human rights and democratic standards of African treaty law, to which Zimbabwe is a signatory. This is what the new pan-Africanism – ushered in by the transition from the Organisation of African Unity to the African Union – is supposed to be about.

Democracy and human rights were at the core of far-reaching reforms to pan-African institutions in the last years of the 20th century. Given the historical memory of subjugation and the reality that contemporary global relations are far from equitable, Africans correctly aspire to define a democratic ethos for their continent. It is well and good that there is a commitment to be African, but surely the quintessence of being African should be about saying "never again" to human rights abuse and assaults on democracy.

Africa has played an important role in the United Nations and in the elaboration of international human rights instruments. Africans have been prominent in articulating alternatives to slavery, colonialism, neo-colonial pillage, structural adjustment programmes, the debt burden, global superpower unilateralism and military adventurism. This tradition of struggle provides the basis for Africa to expand, rather than diminish, the advance of democracy and universal human rights.

The regional leadership challenge

Africa today is no longer lacking in the area of an impressive infrastructure of norms and standards on democratic conduct and human rights observance. President Mbeki and other African leaders have advanced these systems as the *quid pro quo* for the international deals Africa is seeking through international policy platforms and trade meetings – at Gleneagles, Monterrey, Cancun and elsewhere. Granted, the West is by no means a beacon of morality, but it is surely cynical for African leaders to stall the advance of these reforms in protest against unfair terms of trade or unequal voting rights at the Bretton Woods institutions.

The devil is in the praxis. In this regard, the SADC should not allow Mugabe to indulge in the warped and self-serving rhetoric that claims Zimbabwe's elections satisfy the SADC Principles and Guidelines on Democratic Elections, agreed at Grand Baie, Mauritius, in August 2004.

These principles are compromised because they are legally subordinate to the national processes, laws and constitutions of SADC member states.[2] Election monitors, for example, are merely optional. According to the regional principles, monitoring takes place only "in the event a member state decides to extend an invitation to SADC to observe its elections".

The principles require political parties to accept all election results "proclaimed to have been free and fair by the competent national electoral authorities in accordance with the law of the land". There is no caveat about how those authorities are to be chosen in the first place, nor what standards should constitute a democratic minimum for the "law of the land".

Thus, Zimbabwe's elections have been accepted as free and fair, in defiance of the SADC's own parliamentarians. A regional Parliamentary Forum – made up of more than 2,000 southern African legislators – declared Zimbabwe's March 2002 elections to be fraudulent. Their verdict earned them a one-way ticket home.

Similarly, the African Commission on Human and People's Rights has condemned Zimbabwe – apparently to no avail. Civil society entities across the region – trade unions in South Africa, lawyers in Mozambique and Namibia, university students in Swaziland – have demonstrated against abuses perpetrated in Zimbabwe.

Building critical mass
African leaders are not deaf to the moral urgency of these protests. To be sure, there is a growing consciousness that Mugabe does not represent the future that Africa seeks for itself. Zimbabwe's president is falling out of step with a critical mass of thinking among African leaders.

In March 2007, as opposition leaders in Zimbabwe were beaten in police custody, President Festus Mogae was preparing to open a workshop of African parliamentarians in Kasane, Botswana. Drawing on the dignity of his native culture, Mogae observed that there is a saying in Setswana: "the cure of a word is to speak it".

African luminaries such as Desmond Tutu, Nelson Mandela and Kofi Anan have admonished their peers, emphasising that Africans should not pull themselves down into the caricature of self-plundering buffoons. President Mogae made a similar case, some years ago, when he translated another Setswana phrase to journalists who remarked on his choice of a scheduled commercial flight for an official presidential trip. "No individual can see the top of her own head," he told reporters. The proverb is a counsel for humility.

Ghanaian president, John Kufuor, speaking in his capacity as chairman of the African Union, is "embarrassed" by events in Zimbabwe. Zambian president, Levy Mwanawasa, described Zimbabwe as a sinking *Titanic* – a Eureka moment regrettably not sustained. Tanzanian president, Jakaya Kikwete, says dialogue with the opposition is necessary. In contrast, Mugabe talks of "bashing" his opposition. Bishops within his own Catholic Church, alarmed by his choice of words, reproach him for language verging on hate-speech.

Self-interest is another incentive for change. In 2010, South Africa hosts the football World Cup. The event is an opportunity to advertise the competencies of post-apartheid southern Africa and organisers are mindful that another flawed election in Zimbabwe would cast a shadow over their achievement.

Policy makers in Africa no longer dispute the wider ramifications of misrule in Zimbabwe: Harare owes unpaid electricity bills to Mozambique, South Africa and the Democratic Republic of Congo. Its humanitarian crisis has spilled across borders onto the doorsteps of neighbouring countries. Impatience with Mugabe's politics has been openly expressed in Kenya, Nigeria and Senegal.

The route to constitutional reform
What then can Africa do to facilitate a meaningful – in the sense of what I would call a transformative – transition in Zimbabwe? As a first step, African leaders must:
• Disallow the pretense that their continent is supportive of torture, abductions and other human rights abuses.
• Distinguish clearly between expressions of solidarity with Zimbabweans and support for Mugabe and his henchmen.
• Refuse Mugabe's claim that "those who matter" – Zimbabwe's neighbours – are behind him.

As Zimbabwe moves towards parliamentary and presidential elections scheduled for 2008, the SADC must avoid pronouncements which dilute Africa's renewed commitment to common, normative standards for human rights and good governance. Leaders need only follow the example of the African Commission on Human and People's Rights and the SADC Parliamentary Forum in calling human rights infractions by their name.

The regional initiative to agree on an economic rescue package for Zimbabwe must follow a new democratic constitution, and not the other way round. Any other condition will merely allow Mugabe's small band of super-Zimbabweans to capture the benefits of external aid. These are the same elite group who, in the boast of the wife of Zimbabwe's Defence Forces commander, already claim they are "gonna live forever".

The only sustainable solution to the Zimbabwean crisis is constitutional reform. Although mediators led by Mbeki favour this route, it does not empower ordinary citizens to limit the possibilities of a negotiated transition to closet "talks" between a few men who are able to fly between Pretoria and Harare. Leaders, in the widest sense of the term, could urgently convene a national conference of professional and peasant representatives, youth organisations, women's organisations, faith-based movements, political parties and many others to frame a transitional constitution. Its fundamental principles should include interim provisions for non-partisan control of government and the security forces, and a guarantee of free political and campaigning activity.

If the borders imposed on us by the Berlin conference of 1885 have become barriers to our hearing the torment of other Africans, the anti-colonial struggle was in vain. African leaders must no longer remain silent when the next un-medicated child dies in the ghettoes of Zimbabwe, or when the next activist is tortured by secret police in Harare. Only the silence of the world enables such torments, as the Nobel Peace laureate Elie Wiesel eloquently remarked: "Neutrality helps the oppressor, never the victim. Silence encourages the tormentor, never the tormented...When human lives are endangered, when human dignity is in jeopardy, national borders and sensitivities become irrelevant."[3]

Tawanda Mutasah *is a Zimbabwean lawyer and executive director of the Open Society Initiative for Southern Africa.*

The upside-down view of Africa

Opponents of the liberation struggle in Rhodesia have cast themselves as defenders of democracy in Zimbabwe, argues South African president **Thabo Mbeki** *in this edited extract from the online newsletter* ANC Today.

"In his book *Decolonising the Mind*, the Kenyan writer, Ngugi waThiong'o, writes about the consternation among some Europeans that he had started writing in his native language, Gikuyu. He says:

"It was almost as if, in choosing to write in Gikuyu, I was doing something abnormal. The very fact that what common sense dictates in the literary practice of other cultures is questioned in an African writer is a measure of how far imperialism has distorted the view of African realities. It has turned reality upside down: the abnormal is viewed as normal and the normal is viewed as abnormal. Africa actually enriches Europe, but Africa is made to believe that it needs Europe to rescue it from poverty. Africa's natural and human resources continue to develop Europe and America, but Africa is made to feel grateful for aid from the same quarters that still sit on the back of the continent. Africa even produces intellectuals who now rationalise this upside-down way of looking at Africa."

For example, those who fought for a democratic Zimbabwe, with thousands paying the supreme price during the struggle, and forgave their oppressors and torturers in a spirit of national reconciliation, have been turned into repugnant enemies of democracy. Those who, in the interest of their white "kith and kin", did what they could to deny the people of Zimbabwe their liberty, for as long as they could, have become the eminent defenders of the democratic rights of the people of Zimbabwe.

In his book *Diplomacy*, Dr Henry Kissinger discusses the place of the issue of human rights in the East-West struggle during the Cold War. He writes that:

"Reagan and his advisers invoked human rights to try to undermine the Soviet system. To be sure, his immediate predecessors had also affirmed the importance of human rights. Reagan and his advisers went a step further by treating human rights as a tool for overthrowing communism and democratising the Soviet Union. At Westminster in 1982, Reagan, hailing the tide of democracy around the world, called on free nations 'to foster the infrastructure of democracy, the system of a free press, unions, political parties, universities, which allows a people to choose their own way, to develop their own culture, to reconcile their own differences through peaceful means.' America would not wait passively for free institutions to evolve."

In time, and in the interest of "kith and kin", the core of the challenge facing the people of Zimbabwe has disappeared from public view. Its place has been taken by the issue of human rights. Those who have achieved this miracle are not waiting passively for free institutions to evolve.

It is clear that some within Zimbabwe and elsewhere in the world, including our country, are following the example set by "Reagan and his advisers", to "treat human rights as a tool" for overthrowing the government of Zimbabwe and rebuilding Zimbabwe as they wish. In modern parlance, this is called regime change."

The blame game

Regional mediation offers the best prospect of an economic recovery, new constitution and fair elections in Zimbabwe. Despite the obvious limits of SADC influence, writes **Peter Kagwanja**, *African leaders need international support for their initiative.*

A verbal clash between presidents Robert Mugabe and George W. Bush at the UN General Assembly reveals how little progress has been made after seven years of international feuding over Zimbabwe. In a fiery speech to the UN General Assembly in September 2007, Mugabe accused Bush of "rank hypocrisy". A day earlier, the American president had urged the UN Security Council to act against tyranny in Harare.

The incident confirmed Mugabe's transformation in western eyes. Now demonised as an archetypal bare-knuckled tyrant, President Robert Mugabe is a pariah. In a previous era, he was hailed by former British prime minister Margaret Thatcher as "a man I can do business with." Queen Elizabeth II bestowed on him an honorary Knight Commander of the Order of the Bath, in 1994. The metamorphosis from hero to villain has exposed a new "civilisational" fault-line which undermines efforts to find a solution.

The task of mediating between Mugabe and his western foes lies squarely with Zimbabwe's neighbours. In March 2007, the Southern African Development Community (SADC) launched a new initiative to bail Zimbabwe out of its economic woe. South African president Thabo Mbeki was mandated to find a negotiated settlement to a crisis which has imperilled regional stability.

New labour, new problem
Regional mediation offers the best chance of resolving a complex crisis, but Mbeki's initiative has no chance of success unless Africa and the western world tone down their rhetoric. Against this backdrop, the stance assumed in 1997 by Britain's New Labour government was plainly injudicious. The denial by Labourites of Britain's colonial responsibility for land reform in Zimbabwe is blamed for touching off the conflagration.

In 1997, Tony Blair's incoming government reneged on Britain's pledge to fund land reform. The move halted the "willing buyer / willing seller" arrangement, in place since independence, on the grounds that the initial stipend of £44 million allocated by Thatcher's Conservative government had merely oiled cronyism rather than helping the cause of Zimbabwe's landless poor.

The Labourites had effectively gone back on an agreement reached at Lancaster House, where the terms of Zimbabwe's independence were brokered during constitutional negotiations in London in 1979. Zambia's former president, Kenneth Kaunda, recalls that these talks enjoined the incoming black government in Harare to leave the issues of land "in the hands of the British government".

Clare Short, then Britain's minister for international development, set the tone for the dispute in a letter to Zimbabwe's minister of agriculture and land. "I should make it clear that we do not accept that Britain has a special responsibility to meet the costs of land purchase in Zimbabwe," she wrote. "We are a new government from diverse backgrounds without links to former colonial interests. My own origins are Irish and, as you know, we were colonised not colonisers."

The furious response from Harare became apparent in the Fast Track land reform and a string of knee-jerk policies, setting off the fastest peace-time economic dip since Weimar Germany. Zimbabwe suffers from unemployment of more than 80%, collapsed services, annual inflation estimated to reach 18,000% in 2007, and four million people threatened by starvation. The economic situation has spiralled into a regional security concern, triggering an exodus of at least three million refugees.

A nationalist onslaught

Zimbabwe has lost an economic war, but Mugabe appears to have won every political battle with the West. Fearful of western-sponsored "regime change", his government has embarked on an intense militarisation of the country's institutions ahead of elections expected in 2008. At least 40 controlling positions in parastatal organisations are now in the hands of military officials, whose influence has given rise to talk of a "creeping coup" by the military.

In mid-2005, Mugabe launched "Operation *Murambatsvina*" (Drive Out the Filth), a forced clearance of what it termed "illegal shelters" in Harare and other cities. The campaign curbed speculation about prospects for a Ukrainian-style "Orange Revolution" by disrupting the networks of support for the opposition in urban areas. The United Nations estimates that the homes of 700,000 Zimbabweans were destroyed, and the livelihoods of a further 2.4 million adversely affected.

Zimbabwe's real impact in Africa is ideological. In the aftermath of the Iraq invasion in 2003, Mugabe and his allies have sought to defend their cause in terms of an anti-imperial struggle: "Our cause is Africa's cause," he told the fervently pro-Zimbabwe publication, *New African*, in May 2007. Confrontation with the West has emboldened Mugabe's claim to be an icon of African resistance, at once a liberation hero and a victim of racially-inspired retribution for seizing white farms for black Zimbabweans.

Fears of a domino effect in South Africa and Namibia have weighed on the response by neighbouring states to the land seizures in Zimbabwe. Across southern Africa, the vast majority of the black populace continue to feel the effects of historical injustices in racially skewed access to resources and opportunities, particularly land. As the oldest freedom fighter still in office, Mugabe draws the loudest applause on arrival at African meetings – including the SADC summit in Lusaka in August 2007.

The limits of a regional power

Western diplomats have goaded South Africa to break ranks by adopting a more forceful stance on Harare, but brinkmanship has narrowed down the policy choices available to Mbeki and the leadership of his African National Congress.

There is no military option for Pretoria, after the hard lessons of their 1998 military invasion to restore democracy in Lesotho. The incident provoked South Africa's regional neighbours and risked isolating its government. Open criticism from Pretoria of illiberal governments, notably Sani Abacha's Nigeria in the 1990s, precipitated a personal attack on the country's new ANC ministers: South Africa risks being vilified as "the West's lackey on the southern tip of Africa".

Unable to stamp its authority as a regional hegemon, South Africa has pursued what its critics chide as a "quiet diplomacy" policy. Public condemnation of Mugabe's excesses from Pretoria would exacerbate internal rivalries as the ANC prepares to nominate a successor to President Thabo Mbeki. But officials are also deeply wary of the heavy cost of a failed state on Pretoria's doorstep.

In large measure, "quiet diplomacy" has shielded Zimbabwe from international action. Between 2000 and 2004, behind-the-scenes mediation by South Africa yielded a new constitutional draft for Zimbabwe. This initiative – supported by members of both ZANU-PF and the opposition MDC – was stillborn because Pretoria lacked authority to enforce it. Mbeki, in his mid-60s, has had a rough time persuading the octogenarian Mugabe to take him seriously.

Issues of national sovereignty are highly sensitive and often vexed. In a bid for economic leverage, South Africa offered a US$500m credit line to pay Zimbabwe's debt to the International Monetary Fund – on condition that Zimbabwe work to improve governance. The offer was rejected by Harare, where Reserve Bank governor Gideon Gono has scraped together sufficient local resources to fund some of Zimbabwe's external debt.

In February 2006, Mugabe accused officials from Pretoria of conspiring with the British to "use the fact of our owing the IMF to bring about the change of the regime here, squeezing us economically, so politically." The incident sparked a brief episode of what has been termed "megaphone diplomacy". Tito Mboweni, governor of the South African Reserve Bank, declared that "the wheels have come off" in Zimbabwe. Aziz Pahad, deputy foreign minister, warned of dangerous consequences from "the deteriorating economic situation".

Larger than the SADC

While regional leaders may disagree with him in private, few have had the courage to take Mugabe on in public. President Festus Mogae of Botswana has blamed Zimbabwe's woes on a "drought of leadership", but hastily retreated by calling on the West "to supplement what we are already doing". Zambian president Levy Mwanawasa described Zimbabwe as a "sinking Titanic", but made a U-turn in his subsequent role as the SADC chairman by suggesting that the country's problems were "exaggerated". In the words of a senior South African official, "Mugabe is larger than the SADC".

The 14-member bloc has insisted that a solution to Zimbabwe's problems is essential to its economic development plans. In March 2007, an extraordinary meeting was convened after attacks on opposition leaders in Harare. The meeting expressed "solidarity" with Mugabe, and appointed Mbeki to mediate on behalf of the SADC grouping. A subsequent meeting of regional leaders in Lusaka, in August, attempted to negotiate an economic blueprint to pull Zimbabwe from the brink.

Zimbabwe has formidable allies in Namibia and Angola. The trio jointly deployed troops to the Democratic Republic of Congo in 1997, where President Laurent Kabila faced a rebel incursion from the east. Rumours circulated widely in the wake of unrest in Harare's townships following the arrest and beating of MDC leaders in March 2007, that Angola was ready to send in 2,500 paramilitary police (dubbed "Ninjas") to support the Zimbabwean police force.

These favours are reciprocal and historic. In 1999, Angolan president José dos Santos was helped by Zimbabwe to suppress rebel Union of the Total Liberation of Angola (UNITA) forces. Their record of cooperation has made the trio a formidable component of the SADC brigade, launched in August as part of the African Union's Stand-by Force (ASF).

Other African forums could wield influence. The bi-annual summits of African Union heads of state, and the AU Peace and Security Council see Zimbabwe as a "hot potato", but ideological and personality differences have impeded action. Outrage sparked by the *Murambatsvina* slum clearances forced African Union chairman Alpha Konare to send an envoy, but Harare sent him home. Former Mozambican president Joachim Chissano was appointed to mediate in talks with the MDC and was promptly snubbed.

The AU Commission on Human and People's Rights (ACHPR) successfully tabled reports highly critical of the human rights situation in Zimbabwe, to little effect. An alternative, potentially more useful, framework for the African Union is a "Panel of the Wise" composed of five senior Africans tasked with conflict prevention. They could endorse the SADC initiative.

After sanctions

About 200 Zimbabwean government officials and their spouses are affected by a travel ban and asset freeze imposed in 2002 by the European Union, United States and Australia. These have been widely viewed in Africa as racially inspired reprisals for land seizures. Western aid agencies have maintained the flow of humanitarian aid, insisting that the sanctions are designed to discomfort those in power without adding to the suffering of ordinary citizens.

Be that as it may, sanctions have compounded the isolation of Mugabe's regime and fostered an international climate dangerously hostile to Zimbabwe's economic recovery. Given the failure of sanctions to secure any change in policy, western governments should seriously consider throwing their weight behind the SADC.

The Commonwealth Heads of Government Meeting in Kampala, in November 2007, is an opportunity for regional leaders to bring Zimbabwe back onto the agenda. The Commonwealth Secretariat should consider sending a panel of eminent persons, involving prominent Africans and technical experts from other member countries, to explore new ways of supporting the SADC mediation. The regional strategy to devise an economic recovery plan and to re-engage in the process of land reform is worthy of serious attention and encouragement.

Leaders from Europe and Africa are due to meet in December 2007 at the EU-Africa summit in Lisbon, Portugal. British prime minister Gordon Brown will boycott the meeting if President Mugabe attends, as seems likely. President Hifikepunye Pohamba, of Namibia, has vowed to stay away if Mugabe is not invited, an example which other SADC leaders would follow. This stand-off casts a dark cloud over the first EU-Africa summit since 2000. In its role as EU president, Portugal must stand by its decision to invite Zimbabwe's president. The event has the potential to renew ties between the two continents.

The SADC initiative would benefit from endorsement by the UN secretary-general, Ban Ki-Moon. The UN provides a forum for bridging international divisions over Zimbabwe, although clamour for a "UN-backed solution" from western lobbies such as the International Crisis Group is largely unhelpful. Many Africans see attempts by Britain and its allies to raise the issue of Zimbabwe at the UN Security Council as a way of reining in Mugabe. South Africa, a permanent member, maintains the crisis is more about "economic and governance" failures than an issue of human rights.

Influential global elders have more to do. Former presidents Sam Nujoma of Namibia and Kenneth Kaunda of Zambia – Mugabe's contemporaries in the liberation struggles of southern Africa – should work with Europe's new leadership, Gordon Brown and French president Nicolas Sarkozy, to support the SADC mediation. Their priorities must be to deliver an economic recovery plan, a democratic constitution and a level playing field in the elections of 2008.

Dr **Peter Kagwanja** *is acting executive director of the Democracy and Governance programme at the Human Science Research Council in Pretoria, and president of the Africa Policy Institute in Nairobi, Kenya.*

The ABC of fair elections

Regional leaders have failed to coordinate their efforts to bring about free and fair elections in Zimbabwe, argues **Muna Ndulo**. *What happens on polling day is only a small part of a bigger process.*

Zimbabwe is scheduled to hold presidential and parliamentary general elections next year. The Southern African Development Community (SADC) has delegated the task of ensuring that the elections are free and fair and mediating the Zimbabwean crisis to President Thabo Mbeki of South Africa. But the conditions for holding free and fair elections in Zimbabwe do not exist.

Free and fair elections can only be held in an environment which:
- Allows popular participation.
- Promotes human rights.
- Guarantees fundamental freedoms.
- Protects and respects political pluralism.
- Ensures accountability of the government, freedom of the judiciary, and freedom of the press.

None of these conditions exists in Zimbabwe today, nor are they likely to exist by March 2008 in the absence of decisive action to bring them about.

Only serious and determined efforts can move Zimbabwe out of its present quagmire. Contradictory statements about the Zimbabwean situation coming out of the SADC capitals do not inspire any confidence. There is a real risk that these efforts will end up promoting an electoral process whose singular achievement will be to legitimise the Mugabe government.

The international community has often intervened in national election processes through the monitoring of elections. The United Nations has increasingly been called upon to monitor national elections in many parts of the world including South Africa, Namibia and Mozambique. Other intergovernmental organisations such as the European Union, the Commonwealth and the African Union, and a considerable number of non-governmental organisations are also active in the field.

Such involvement can only be effective if it involves participation in the whole spectrum of the national election process. It has to include:

- Support of national election administrations.
- Training of election officials.
- Election supervision.
- Election observation.
- Election verification.
- Provision of civilian police.
- Technical assistance on election-related matters.

There is an absolute need to ensure that the 2008 elections in Zimbabwe are not only free and fair but are seen to be free and fair, if they are to be accepted by all political factions as well as by the outside world. But the circumstances under which the elections are to be held present huge challenges. These include the pervasive lack of political tolerance and the prevalence of political violence; high levels of intimidation and bias; and the memory that previous elections have been marred by violence and serious electoral irregularities. There are also logistical concerns. The previous elections were characterised by selective voter registration and gerrymandering of electoral districts.

The situation is heightened by an institutional culture which tolerates a profound disrespect for human rights. The police and the army are often used by the Government to frustrate free political activity. This makes the police unsuitable to guard polling stations and to perform functions such as transporting ballot papers without supervision.

Preparing the ground

In order that the international community's involvement is not seen as legitimising a flawed election, it is essential for Mr Mbeki's mission to put in place structures that will tackle the above challenges. In the South African process in 1994 special structures such as the Transitional Executive Council (TEC) were established to ensure that the apartheid regime was terminated and did not undermine the transition to democracy.

Mr. Mbeki should not only be interested in what happens on the day of the elections. To reduce the probability of rigging and enhance the integrity of the elections, he should give considerable weight to the conditions on the ground leading up to voting day. Monitoring activity should cover – geographically and chronologically – the entire electoral process, from the initial stages of registration through the elections themselves.

The focus of the international community's involvement in elections is to monitor the elections to ensure that they are free and fair and are run in accordance with internationally accepted election norms, established by the Universal Declaration of Human Rights. Article 21 of the Universal Declaration states that: "everyone has the right to take part in the government of his country, directly or through freely chosen representatives." It adds that: "the will of the people shall be the basis of the authority of government: this will shall be expressed in periodic and genuine elections which shall be by universal and equal suffrage and shall be held by secret vote or by equivalent free voting procedures."

In Namibia in 1989 and Angola in 1992, the United Nations developed and applied standards that moved beyond this limited formula. A consensus developed around what constitutes free and fair elections. The most important of these standards are:
- A right of all voters to participate in the electoral process without hindrance.
- Free campaigning for all political parties.
- Secrecy of the ballot.
- Reasonable speed in the counting of ballots.
- Accountability and openness of the electoral process to the competing parties.
- An acceptable electoral law.

Observance of elections must extend to all actions of a national Electoral Commission. Specifically, the actions of an Electoral Commission must be monitored to verify:
- The extent of freedom of organisation, movement, assembly and expression during the electoral campaign.
- The adequacy of measures taken to ensure that political parties and alliances enjoy those freedoms without hindrance or intimidation.
- Access to media by all political parties contesting the elections.
- Whether voter education efforts of the electoral authorities and other interested parties to educate voters ensure that voters are being adequately informed on both the meaning of the vote and its procedural aspects.
- The registration of voters to ensure that qualified voters are not denied the necessary identification document
- Whether voting occurs on election days in an environment free of intimidation and conditions which ensure free access to voting stations and the secrecy of the vote
- The adequacy of measures taken to ensure the proper transport and custody of ballots, and the security of the vote count.

Reaching a verdict

The final determination is made easier when international observers pronounce their judgment at each stage of the process. There are three main stages in the electoral process: the registration of voters; the campaign period; the voting and the counting of voting. Each of these stages should be certified free and fair before proceeding to the next stage. In this way, the chances of a disputed outcome of the election are minimized. Otherwise the observer exercise becomes superficial and its conclusions either vague or empirically untenable.

This raises two difficult questions for Mbeki. How is he going to ensure that the conditions outlined above are met? What structure is the SADC going to put in place to ensure that the conditions are implemented? It appears that the SADC strategy is to achieve reform by persuading Mugabe to dismantle the autocratic and repressive system he has established. If indeed that is the strategy, the SADC initiative is bound to fail.

One of the lessons to be learnt out of the recent disgraceful Nigerian elections is that undemocratic regimes cannot reform themselves. The Mugabe government will not democratise unless pushed. It has no desire to be open. There are transaction costs to running an open system of governance. For a corrupt and autocratic government these costs could trigger its demise.

The role of the international community will be critical to the outcome of the regional mediation in Zimbabwe. A united approach to a conflict greatly increases the chances of successful intervention. South Africa and Mozambique are among the best examples of the positive role a united international community can play. Many other international conflicts have been worsened when countries with different objectives have supported different factions, or when the political attention span of states does not reach far beyond polling day.

Muna Ndulo *is professor of law at Cornell University Law School, New York. He has acted as a political and legal adviser to UN missions in South Africa and East Timor, and as special representative of the secretary-general in South Africa.*

The old bogey

Concern for Zimbabwe has stirred deep and racially charged anxieties. **Ronald Suresh Roberts** *argues that among white liberals, knee-jerk caricatures have taken the place of honest analysis.*

The word "Zimbabwe" is the Pavlovian Bell of the white South African mind. Once the word rings out, all remnants of liberal good sense retreat, replaced by salivation and loud barking. Consider Helen Suzman, interviewed by the London *Weekend Telegraph* under the headline "Democracy? It was better under apartheid, says Helen Suzman". You might think, reading this, that Suzman was talking about South Africa and seeking a return to its apartheid past but her thoughts were dominated by Robert Mugabe rather than South Africa. "For all my criticisms of the current [South African] system, it doesn't mean that I would like to return to the old one. I don't think we will ever go the way of Zimbabwe, but people are entitled to be concerned. I am hopeful about any future for whites in this country – but not entirely optimistic."

The headline was flatly contradicted by the quoted content of the interview. Something more than incompetence was at work here: the headline felt right, despite its obvious contradiction of the interview, because Zimbabwe indeed operates in the colonial subconscious as an alter ego for South Africa itself. Most South African discourse on Zimbabwe is less about Zimbabwe and more about South African and colonial whites granting themselves permission to indulge in dystopian nightmares that are starkly at odds with the new South African realities. Zimbabwe ceases to exist as a country with a people and a politics of its own. It becomes a prism through which apartheid liberals project their deepest and darkest – especially darkest – South African preoccupations.

The dyspeptic *Mail & Guardian* columnist, Robert Kirby, regularly wrote of a fictionalised character called "Thabob Mugabeki", a troll who occasionally darts out from under his presidential bridge "to frighten passing Europeans" and whose subjects are accustomed to being "clubbed to death for not starving quickly enough." Such a composite figure operates, in all seriousness, throughout the white South African discourse of Zimbabwe. The name itself, Mugabeki, decorates the racist blogosphere while R.W. Johnson identifies something he terms "Mugabe-Mbeki speak." Rhoda Kadalie claims to have discovered for South Africans what she calls "our own internal Zimbabwe." William Gumede, in his usual self-contradictory style, has suggested that "although the ANC in South Africa and Zanu-PF are light years apart, the spectre of 'Zanufication' haunts South Africa." And, of course, Zwelinzima Vavi: "We may be on our way to the Zimbabwean crisis in the long run."

…To the unsubstantiated bogey of an "anti-white" Mbeki, Suzman added: "Mugabe has destroyed that country while South Africa has stood by and done nothing. The way Mugabe was fêted at the inauguration last month was an embarrassing disgrace. But it served well to illustrate very clearly Mbeki's point of view." Mugabe attended the 2004 inauguration and was enthusiastically greeted by the crowd in attendance but he was not "fêted" by Mbeki, nor did Suzman clarify how the crowd's response might "illustrate very clearly Mbeki's point of view." All such chatter is less about the real problems of Zimbabwe than about the conscious and subconscious fears, resentments, jealousies and desires for the historical vindication of white South Africa. The quest is not to solve Zimbabwe's problems but the fear of racial "contagion" by them.

Two years after Suzman's comments, *Business Day* reported that "President Mbeki has reached new heights of popularity, with last year's job-approval ratings matching those the public last gave to his predecessor, Nelson Mandela." The war against such realities necessarily relies upon the liberals' traditional weapon of stereotype. As Ken Owen has noticed: "Zimbabwe has become a pretext for renewed demands for President Thabo Mbeki to 'do something', failing which he is to be denounced as unfit to govern."

From Ronald Suresh Roberts, *Fit to Govern: The Native Intelligence of Thabo Mbeki* (p152-4) STE Publishers, South Africa.

Between an ostrich and a flamingo

Frank discussion among adversaries helped influential South Africans to overcome their differences in the last years of apartheid. **Adam Kahane** *asks whether the same effort is needed in Zimbabwe.*

In the twilight years of apartheid, a diverse group of South Africans convened at the Mont Fleur conference centre near Cape Town. Over the course of four intense but informal weekends, they talked through what was happening in South Africa, what might happen and what, in the light of these possible futures, could be done.

These days, I read the news from Zimbabwe with alarm and confusion. I observe a downward spiral of fear, mistrust and violence. I notice a narrow focus on the current crisis and its personalities, and widely differing perspectives on what has gone wrong. I wonder if Zimbabweans can jointly agree on what should be done about it. Then I think back to that meeting near Cape Town.

The "Mont Fleur Process", which I facilitated, brought together a broad mix of South African political, business and civil society leaders. They came from the Left and Right, the opposition and the government – among them Dorothy Boesak, Rob Davies, Derek Keys, Pieter le Roux, Johann Liebenberg, Saki Macozoma, Mosebyane Malatsi, Trevor Manuel, Vincent Maphai, Tito Mboweni, Jayendra Naidoo, Brian O'Connell, Viviene Taylor, Sue van der Merwe and Christo Wiese. In different ways, all exerted influence to shape how the future subsequently unfolded.

Scenario planning

From starkly different perspectives, they built a shared map of the reality of their country at that time. A summary of their discussions was published in July 1992 by the *Mail and Guardian* newspaper, in the form of four stories. Each scenario imagined how events might unfold over the coming decade:

- *Ostrich* told the story of a non-representative white government sticking its head in the sand to try – ultimately in vain – to avoid a negotiated settlement with the black majority.
- *Lame Duck* anticipated a prolonged transition under a weak government which, because it purports to respond to all, satisfies none.
- *Icarus*, a constitutionally unconstrained black government comes to power on a

wave of popular support and noble intentions, and embarks on a huge and unsustainable public spending programme which crashes the economy.
* *Flight of the Flamingos* portrayed a successful transition from apartheid, with everyone in the society rising slowly and together.

These stories may not be relevant to either South Africa or Zimbabwe today. But they reflected key choices facing South African leaders at the time. They emphasised the nature of various possible political settlements and the economic policies that would follow. Of the four scenarios, history since 1992 has been closest – although certainly not identical – to *Flight of the Flamingos*.

The more significant lesson, however, is not in the scenario stories but in the process itself. The structure of those weekend sessions is typical of one of the most important innovations of South Africa's transition: the multi-stakeholder dialogue forum. From 1990 onwards, South Africans created – in parallel with the formal negotiating structures – hundreds of such informal forums.

These dealt with a variety of challenges – local development, health, education, security, constitutional reform. Some adopted the scenarios method. More importantly, all created a safe and open space in which the primary political, business, and civil society actors could come together to chart a way forward.

A safe and open space
The key concept here is "we" – an assumption of shared interests and identity which, at first, was often denied. The forums encouraged a sense of South Africans being engaged in a shared national project. The old was not yet dead and the new had not yet been born. In this *interregnum*, the forums provided a space for the people with a stake in the future to create it together.

The sense of incremental trust – "we" – was a foundation for the larger political settlement in 1994 and the transformation which followed. "There was a high degree of flux at that time," recalled Trevor Manuel, who later became South Africa's minister of finance. "That was a real strength. There was no paradigm, there was no precedent, there was nothing. We had to *carve* it, and so perhaps we were more willing to listen."

Since Mont Fleur, I have facilitated similar future-carving processes in other conflicts. In Colombia during the civil war: in Guatemala after the genocide: in Argentina during the collapse; in Northern Ireland, Cyprus, Israel-Palestine, India and the Philippines; and in my homeland of Canada, with its own hidden deep differences.

Sometimes these processes work and sometimes they don't – as Immanuel Kant said: "Out of the crooked timber of humanity, no straight thing was ever made." When they do, it is always because there are a few people who are willing to take a stand, not for a particular interest, but for a process which is open-minded and open-hearted: for carving a better future.

Tempers flare over recovery plan

A report of a rift between regional leaders at their summit in Lusaka in August 2007 prompted an angry response from South African president, Thabo Mbeki. In a follow-up article, Business Day newspaper stuck by its story that Mugabe dismissed the SADC's economic strategy for Zimbabwe.

SADC leaders "divided on Zimbabwe crisis"

By Dumisani Muleya, Business Day, August 20th 2007

Southern African Development Community (SADC) leaders were sharply divided at last week's tense summit in Zambia on how to deal with Zimbabwe's political and economic crises.

The regional leaders were for the most part at odds over Zimbabwe's controversial economic report...The rift was triggered by differences over the analysis and prognosis of the report compiled by SADC executive secretary, Tomaz Augusto, which has stringent conditions for Zimbabwe's proposed economic rescue package.

The conditions to the "take-it-or-leave-it" deal sparked resistance from Harare authorities, while other SADC leaders felt the report was a fair assessment of economic circumstances in Zimbabwe.

Due to the rupture, the report was merely noted - not adopted - and sent back to finance ministers so they could draw up an economic rescue plan in consultation with the Zimbabwean government.

The preconditions to aid for Zimbabwe included the need for political and legal reforms, economic liberalisation and privatisation of public enterprises.

SADC proposed sending economic advisers and monitors to oversee the implementation of the economic rescue programme.

Complete fiction

By Thabo Mbeki, ANC Today, August 24th 2007

On Monday August 20th the Business Day newspaper published a wholly fabricated story alleging that the SADC leaders were divided, describing a discussion at the Summit Meeting that never took place. This is consistent with an unethical practice in sections of our media in terms of which they manufacture news and information and communicate complete fiction as the truth.

The newspaper manufactured an unbridgeable

I do not understand what is going on in Zimbabwe well enough to know if these experiences are relevant there. Do Zimbabweans have a sense of a common future, of a "we"? Do the primary actors from politics, business and civil society know that they need each other? Or that they need even their opponents, to create a better future? What I do understand – and with certainty – is what happens if the answers to these questions are "No". Because the only alternative then is that some or all of these actors will attempt to impose a future by force.

Adam Kahane *has mediated in conflicts in North and South America, Europe and Asia, and is the author of* Solving Tough Problems *(San Francisco: Berrett-Koehler, 2004).*

"rift" resulting in a non-existent paralysis among the leaders, arising out of the discussion that never took place. The fact of the matter is that, acting on the recommendation of the SADC Organ on Politics, Defence and Security, (the Organ), the SADC Summit Meeting accepted the report on the Zimbabwe economy, as well as the proposal of the Organ that our Finance Ministers, in consultation with the Government of Zimbabwe, should use the report to elaborate specific interventions that could be made by our region.

Mugabe tantrum at SADC comes to light

By Dumisani Muleya, *Business Day,*
September 7th 2007

Zimbabwean president, Robert Mugabe, stormed out of the recent Southern African Development Community (SADC) summit after an explosive clash with Zambian President Levy Mwanawasa during a closed session, it has emerged.

Upon his return to Zimbabwe, Mugabe said the meeting went well but made it clear his regime would continue with its own programmes, regardless of what the SADC leaders were saying.

Senior SADC diplomats say the trouble started after Mbeki delivered his report on talks between ZANU-PF and the MDC.

"After Mbeki delivered his report to the summit, Mwanawasa, as the chair of the meeting, said there was an urgent need to discuss Zimbabwe because the situation there had become 'unacceptable'. Tanzanian president, Jakaya Kikwete, said there was no need to discuss it because talks were in progress and Mbeki concurred," a senior diplomat said. "Kikwete then suggested Mugabe should be asked what he thought about Mwanawasa's proposal. When Mugabe was given the platform to speak he launched an angry tirade, attacking Mwanawasa left, right and centre before walking out in protest."

The diplomat said Mugabe angrily asked: "Who are you, Mwanawasa? Who are you? Who do you think you are?"

"Mugabe also said he was aware of Mwanawasa's recent meetings with western intelligence agencies on Zimbabwe. He said he would 'not allow Mwanawasa to sell out Zimbabwe as he has done Zambia'," the diplomat said.

"During the process, Mwanawasa was shaken and he kept on saying: 'Mr President I didn't mean to say that; you misunderstood me. No, Mr President, that was not my intention.'"

Sources said Mugabe, after blasting Mwanawasa, walked out and did not return.

Extracted from an article written by Dumisani Muleya for *Business Day*, August 20th 2007 and edited for clarity; from *ANC Today*, Volume 7, No. 33, 24-30 August 2007, and edited for clarity; from *Business Day*, September 7th 2007, and edited for clarity

Rough justice

The breakdown of the post-colonial settlement has triggered mass emigration from Zimbabwe, but across the region democracy is more keenly craved than ever before. On the border with Mozambique, **Mark Ashurst** *observes an unwritten constitution at work.*[1]

The chief of police is all smiles. A big man and jovial, he strides towards us wearing a T-shirt and flip-flops. A large brown bottle of *Dos M* beer dangles from one hand.

The farmer, a white Zimbabwean burnished red by the sun, climbs out of his pick-up. They meet like old friends. They speak Shona, Zimbabwe's mother tongue – the Mozambican is fluent. It's a scene that not long ago was commonplace in Zimbabwe too.

We're in Chimoio, a market town in north-western Mozambique, an hour's drive from Zimbabwe. I've hitched a lift with the farmer, who has left his birthplace outside Harare to start again on a neglected plot of land leased from the government in Maputo.

From my vantage point in the back of his truck I watch their noisy, ebullient exchange. The police chief, noticing me, makes an inscrutable gesture – the joke, apparently, is on me. Beer bellies sag over their shorts, swaying as they laugh.

It turns out that I'm not the first man brought here on the back of the farmer's pick-up into the path of the police chief. The last one was a labourer, caught over-charging for the farmer's tomatoes at the street market.

Six weeks later, the labourer is still locked up at the police station. In return, the police chief enjoys a steady supply of tomatoes - a perk of the job. "Rough justice," I whisper to my friend, Sidonio.

Next to me in the back of the pick-up, Sidonio shrugs. "You have to," he says. Sidonio runs a bar in Maputo, the capital. "I'd do it too if one of my barmen was stealing. You cut a deal with the police chief."

They are pragmatists: Sidonio, the police chief and the farmer. Cutting deals, trading favours, the sum of these transactions adds up to a political process. For practical purposes, this is the unwritten constitution which governs life in a rural and under-developed corner of southern Africa.

The market in Chimoio, capital of the otherwise sparsely populated Manica province, is laden with goods which were once plentiful in Zimbabwe. Packets of food, washing powder and sanitary towels are stacked on the wooden tables. Plastic buckets, sacks of maize and crates of cooking oil line the road.

On the far side of the Mozambican border, the old political order is breaking down. For many Zimbabweans, these basic goods are scarce commodities. Some of the drains which run beneath the outlying shanty towns of Harare (politely known as "high-density suburbs") are blocked with sand. This is not sabotage, like the departing Portuguese settlers who poured concrete into Maputo sewers. Poor people in Harare are washing their pots and pans, even their own bodies, with sand. Hyperinflation has rendered even soap unaffordable.

Strategies for change

Zimbabwe's president, Robert Mugabe, is under pressure from his neighbours to restore stability. The Zimbabwe dollar has collapsed and the Reserve Bank is printing money to pay its bills. Bank notes must be carried in satchels. For the economy to recover, Zimbabwe needs balance of payments support – an injection of hard currency – from the multilateral financial institutions.

The Southern African Development Community (SADC) has urged precisely that course, specifying the kinds of economic policies prescribed, a decade ago, by the International Monetary Fund. Officials in Harare harbour grim memories of that experience and their leader is in no mood to cooperate now.

Not that he is likely to qualify for hard currency, beyond the humanitarian aid already channelled through the Reserve Bank by foreign charities and aid agencies. Access to external credit is controlled, largely, by lending institutions set up by countries whose governments have been among Mugabe's staunchest critics. For Zimbabwe to secure external credit while Mugabe is president would require a bold *volte face* in the boardrooms of the global development industry.

Thabo Mbeki, appointed as mediator by the SADC, has stuck by a more nuanced strategy. He wants a deal between ZANU-PF and the opposition MDC, followed – perhaps not immediately – by an "elegant exit" for Mugabe. At the core of this strategy is an attempt to confer a shred of legitimacy on Zimbabwe's delinquent politics. To the fury of human rights and pro-democracy activists, this so-called "quiet diplomacy" is rooted in suspicion that neither ZANU-PF nor the MDC has a credible programme for change.

Zimbabwe bears all the hallmarks of a colonial state. Its economy depends still on tobacco and farming, although these industries are in disarray after Mugabe's chaotic seizure of white-owned farms. State institutions, from the secret police to government departments, are used and abused by a small clique of officials. The mechanisms of internal repression bear an uncanny resemblance to those on which Ian Smith relied to suppress demands for majority rule during the bloodbath of Rhodesia's civil war. Except that these days, of course, the faces of the securocrats are black, not white.

Even universal schooling, Mugabe's biggest achievement, was built on an education system inherited from colonial times. It seems extraordinary that a man who was once the toast of the liberal world has fashioned a new nation, Zimbabwe, which in its structure and government so closely resembles the old one.

He formed a government of national unity, invited white people to the cabinet table and reassured the commercial farmers. Lovemore Mgibi, a Zimbabwean businessman and academic who left ZANU-PF in 1985, says the spirit of reconciliation was underwritten by a more explicit understanding: "You grow the food," Mugabe told the farmers. "You support our governance. In return, we'll always give you a cabinet seat."

Perhaps this explains why Mugabe was praised in the 1980s as a champion of reconciliation – the Nelson Mandela of his decade. The comparison is dubious, of course: Mugabe's hands are steeped in blood, from the vicious colonial war against the old Rhodesia to the Matabeleland massacres soon after independence. But he was a great conciliator too.

The economic chaos which has engulfed Zimbabwe began with the invasions of commercial farms by a state-sponsored militia, under the leadership of disgruntled war veterans. They had been among Mugabe's detractors, but were deftly deployed against whites only when the president faced a real challenge from a new opposition. The

Movement for Democratic Change is a party bankrolled by sympathisers abroad and the farmers at home. It's a deeply personal quarrel for Mugabe.

Mgibi describes the president's attitude to the farmers in the terms of a modern day revenge tragedy: "You betrayed us. You messed us up. If we go down, you're going down with us."

A new dispensation
Zimbabwe has long been a land of deep, perhaps implacable, suspicions. "Tsvangirai, Mugabe, everyone is mistrusted," Mgibi told me. The politicians summoned by Mbeki to the negotiating table are heirs to a well-established tradition of power-brokers gathering behind closed doors. None can claim to have created a fair society; in Zimbabwe, they failed spectacularly.

The pervasive inequalities of sub-Saharan Africa are a theme to which Mbeki returns time and again. "When the poor rise, they will rise against us all," he warns. Since succeeding Nelson Mandela in 1999, the South African president has positioned himself as the cheerleader for a brave new era of democratic norms and standards for Africa. His government has been the prime mover in constructing a new African Union to replace the atrophied and ineffectual Organisation of African Unity. A New Partnership for African Development (NEPAD), crafted in Pretoria, set a seal of African authorship on a renewed effort to trade improved governance for a new deal on foreign aid and access to markets in the industrialised world.

The fate of Zimbabwe cannot fairly be held up as an acid test of the new institutional architecture which Mbeki advocates for Africa. But nor is the situation in Zimbabwe an entirely separate matter. The Harare government has been a reluctant participant in Mbeki's system, and Mugabe resists any aspect of this putative new order which would diminish national sovereignty.

Instead, the ambiguous signals emerging from regional meetings have exposed the limits of a written constitution in parts of the world governed for too long by unwritten contracts between farmers, police officers and presidents. In pursuit of an orderly settlement, regional leaders have waived the minimum criteria for human rights and the rule of law almost before the ink on various charters of the new African Union had dried. The unambiguous terms in which these new rights are spelt out contrasts bluntly with the cautious diplomacy of African governments.

Sitting on the back of the Zimbabwean farmer's pick-up truck in Mozambique, I wonder what it would take to turn the jovial police chief against the smiling white farmer. A poor crop of tomatoes, perhaps? Another twenty years of slow-burning resentment glossed over with deals, favours, rough justice?

If Zimbabwe's turmoil holds any lesson for Africa, it is that democracy is more keenly craved now than it has ever been. Not because democracy is any remedy for the political and economic inheritance of southern Africa: the labourer in the police cell could vouch for that. But because it promises a better alternative than the old political art that brought peace to post-independence Africa.

Sooner or later a new government will take power in Harare. The new order is likely to bring an unwieldy coalition of rivals and the deal-making, once again, will take place in private. Most Zimbabweans will view the outcome with a deeply engrained scepticism – a characteristic already familiar in most of the world's oldest democracies. That may be no bad thing. Next time, Zimbabweans will not be easily duped.

Mark Ashurst *is director of the Africa Research Institute, London. He has worked in Africa as a journalist for the* Financial Times, Newsweek *and the* BBC.

4. ZIMBABWE AND THE WORLD

British policies have not helped Zimbabwe – yet

Of all Zimbabwe's foreign ties, the relationship with Britain looms large. **Richard Dowden** *argues that by ignoring a history of betrayal, Tony Blair and his ministers played into Mugabe's hands. In future, South Africa and China will wield more influence.*

It began with the double-crossing of Lobengula, the Ndebele King, when Cecil Rhodes' pioneers seized Shona territory to establish Rhodesia in 1890. From the beginning, Britain's dealings with Zimbabwe were marked by duplicity and a callous disregard for its people.

Lobengula's kingdom was destroyed and the land seized for white settlement – a policy that continued until the 1960s. Rhodesia was white man's territory. In 1904 there were 12,500 whites living there, by 1946 the white population had grown to 82,000 and then leapt to 225,000 by 1965. The government in Britain tried to balance the interests of the African population which had grown in that period from under a million to 4.5 million. But it was never willing to deploy more than persuasion against white rule. After the Unilateral Declaration of Independence by whites in 1965, Britain ruled out calls for military pressure on the grounds that diplomats assumed that the rebellion would be over "in weeks rather than months".

Instead, Britain promised sanctions, which were duly broken, or allowed to be broken. The minority regime stayed in power for 14 bloody years, until Britain finally accepted the surrender of Ian Smith's Rhodesian Front at Lancaster House in 1979. But to this day, the precise detail of what was, or was not, promised to the new nation is veiled in controversy.

Many Zimbabweans believed Britain had promised to set up a fund to buy out white land. If this promise was made at all, it can have been little more than a "gentleman's agreement", finessed by the British foreign minister, Lord Carrington. Others have claimed the deal was struck amid hints that £2 billion would be made available later to fund land redistribution.

Whatever the terms, the outcome was to ensure that the vexed issue of land was taken off the table during independence negotiations. The final text of the Lancaster House agreement stated only that land would be transferred from white to black ownership on a willing buyer / willing seller basis.

A decade of good manners

Relations with Britain subsequently calmed. Aid flowed, despite disagreement over African demands for sanctions against apartheid South Africa. In the first few years of Zimbabwe's independence, President Mugabe established a close, if not cordial, relationship with Margaret Thatcher, though their political beliefs could not have been further apart.

Much to the amazement of officials at the prime minister's Downing Street office, Mugabe would drop in for informal chats with Mrs Thatcher during private visits to London. "We always seem to get on better with the Tories than with Labour politicians," Nathan Shamuyarira, the veteran ZANU-PF insider and party spokesman, told me.

The good manners survived the Matabeleland massacres of the early 1980s, when Britain kept quiet and supplied weapons while Mugabe's 5 Brigade killed thousands of Ndebele people. Britain also provided military support to safeguard the Beira corridor – a vital trade route from Zimbabwe to the Indian Ocean coast of Mozambique.

The cooperation had a strategic goal. Britain's strategy to promote change but prevent revolution in South Africa needed Mugabe on board. But British officials badly misread their man, imagining that Mugabe's socialist, anti-capitalist and anti-imperialist rhetoric was largely a tactic deployed for the purposes of the liberation war.

To the British Foreign Office, Mugabe was a pragmatist. Few doubted he would do what he was told when faced with economic pressure or the threat of cuts in foreign aid. When Zimbabwe's economic reform programme went badly off track in the late 1990s, Britain refused to condone any softening of the "Structural Adjustment" policies prescribed by the World Bank and International Monetary Fund.

From insults to injury

In 1997, Tony Blair's Labour government came to power. The first meeting of the two leaders, at the 1997 Commonwealth Conference in Edinburgh, ended in acrimony. Mugabe wanted Blair to provide money to buy out the white farmers. Blair took the view that the past was the past, Zimbabwe was an independent country and Britain's responsibility was at an end.

For Mugabe, under pressure to assert his political gravitas while the economy deteriorated at home, this brush-off by a young English politician who clearly did not know his history was a terrible insult. Mugabe saw himself as a great African leader, but already his reputation had been overshadowed by the rapturous acclaim for his southern neighbour, Nelson Mandela.

Other British cabinet ministers proved equally tactless. Mugabe exploded with rage when Clare Short, then minister for International Development, suggested that her own ancestors in Ireland suffered from colonialism as much as Zimbabwe. Peter Hain, a former activist who claimed to be "of Africa", compounded this resentment by lecturing Mugabe on civilised behaviour.

Still more humiliating was an attempted citizen's arrest of Mugabe by gay rights activist Peter Tatchell, ostensibly in protest at the oppression of homosexuals in Zimbabwe. To this day, Mugabe believes Tatchell's headline-grabbing stunt was carried out on the orders of the British government.

In response, he taunted Blair with accusations that Britain wanted to take over Zimbabwe again. This also suited Mugabe's domestic agenda. He headed off a growing protest movement by "war veterans" from the left by turning them on the white farmers who had funded the opposition Movement for Democratic Change. By seizing the land owned by "Britain's children" in Zimbabwe, Mugabe at a stroke undermined both sources of opposition to his rule.

In 2000 when he found Britain was sending new communications equipment to its Harare High Commission, Mugabe had it seized. Britain responded with rhetorical denunciations and ineffectual sanctions which Mugabe skilfully threw back in Britain's face as neo-colonial bullying. By presenting this feud as a new phase of anti-imperial conflict, Mugabe has attained a certain folk-hero status in parts of Africa.

Lessons for Britain

The last decade has made clear Britain's weakness when it comes to standing up to tyranny in Africa. Among Zimbabweans who suffer from Mugabe's vicious rule, Britain is condemned for not doing enough. Its mean-minded immigration policies frustrated

Zimbabwean asylum seekers, inviting suspicion that Britain's relationship with Zimbabwe remains at least ambiguous, at most duplicitous.

Now, as then, Britain puts its relationship with South Africa before its relationship with Zimbabwe. But Britons in general – and Britain's media in particular – have a strange obsession with Zimbabwe. As a journalist who struggled to interest editors in reports from Congo, Nigeria, Ghana or Kenya, I always knew that I could sell a story about Zimbabwe to an editor.

For all Britain's policy failures, there remains a deep well of goodwill towards Zimbabweans in Britain. Once Mugabe goes, that could be turned into a partnership to rebuild the country. South Africa and China will have replaced Britain as the lead partners but Britain still has a role to play, both as an individual donor and in Europe, to coordinate international assistance.

And it could also devise a system that would allow the thousands of skilled and hard-working Zimbabweans who have settled in Britain to contribute to the rebuilding of their country without losing their rights and status in their new home. That too could be a model for relations between Europe and Africa.

Richard Dowden *is director of the Royal African Society in London. He was formerly Africa editor of* The Economist.

British officals greeted ZANU-PF's landslide victory in the first all-race election of 1980 with tight-lipped surprise. But Lord Carrington made clear that Robert Mugabe was considered unlikely to come under Soviet influence. Cold War loyalties encouraged the cordial relationship which subsequently emerged between Mugabe and Margaret Thatcher.

British Heartened by Rhodesia Voting

Though Mugabe victory provokes some apprehension, officials acclaim election itself

By R.W. Apple Jr.
Special to *The New York Times*

London, March 4 –The British government hailed the success of the Rhodesian elections today while wondering privately and slightly apprehensively about what lay ahead.

The sweeping victory of Robert Mugabe jolted expert opinion here. Although most ministers had looked for a result that would require the formation of a coalition, which they believed most likely to lead to stability, they had concluded in recent days that it would be impossible to exclude Mr. Mugabe. None had been prepared for the possibility that he would win an outright majority.

But both Lord Carrington, the foreign secretary, who was the principal architect of the Lancaster House conference that led to the elections, and his deputy, Sir Ian Gilmour, the Lord Privy Seal, rejected suggestions in parliament this afternoon that Mr. Mugabe, who called himself a Marxist, was in any sense a pawn of the Soviet Union.

In the House of Lords, the Foreign Secretary said that "in point of fact it was from the Chinese that Mr. Mugabe very largely got the weapons" for his guerrilla army. In the House of Commons, Sir Ian went further, saying, "I have no evidence that Mr. Mugabe is under Soviet influence – quite the contrary."

'The Time for Reconciliation'
Nevertheless, Lord Carrington sounded a note of caution amid the congratulations flooding in upon him. In a notably restrained speech, he told the peers, and the Rhodesians, that "now is the time for reconciliation, hope and encouragement that all those who fought in the election will learn to work together."

"Congratulations are only due," he added, "when we see that the outcome of this has been a free and fair multiracial society operating in peaceful conditions."

In a brief statement, prime minister Margaret Thatcher refrained from congratulating Mr. Mugabe, as did Lord Carrington. The only member of the government to do so was Sir Ian, and he acted only under the pressure of Labour members of parliament. They were delighted by Mr. Mugabe's victory, seeing it as justification for their refusal, when in office, to recognise Bishop Abel T. Muzorewa, the prime minister in the biracial government that resigned to allow the new elections.

Mrs. Thatcher declared: "I think the most appropriate thing I can do is to say that the arrangement of free and fair elections under all the circumstances have been an outstanding achievement, which many, a few months ago, would have thought impossible. The Governor is to be congratulated. So is the army, the monitoring force and the police. The object was to arrange these elections. It was for the people of Rhodesia to say exactly who they wished to have."

Only a few discordant voices were heard, and among those, the loudest was that of Julian Amery, a Conservative backbencher with right-wing views on foreign policy who often clashes with the leadership of his party. Mr. Amery charged that Mr. Mugabe's victory was a major defeat for the West, comparable to that in Afghanistan.

This article was first published in the *New York Times,* March 5th 1980.

Small fish in a Chinese sea

The solidarity nurtured by Chairman Mao with ZANU-PF is waning, but it's not too late to negotiate a new role for Zimbabwe in Chinese plans for Africa. From Beijing, **Lindsey Hilsum** *sees the opportunity for a tough bargain.*

Alphabetical misfortune dictated that the President of Zimbabwe should be the last African leader to shake the hand of the Chinese president, Hu Jintao.

Robert Mugabe cut a sorry figure, loping across the reception room in the Great Hall of the People as the cameras whirred for the 42nd time. Once he had been a special guest, awarded an Honorary Professorship at Beijing's Foreign Affairs University. But at the Africa Summit in November 2006, he was just one amongst dozens craving Chinese investment, loans, aid and political support.

Celebrating 25 years of Zimbabwe's independence in 2005, Mugabe announced: "We have turned east where the sun rises and given our backs to the west, where the sun sets." After the EU and US withdrew all except emergency aid, he believed China would rescue Zimbabwe.

In his dotage, Mugabe sees the events of thirty years ago more vividly than the present. He characterises Chinese interest in Zimbabwe as the actions of a friend in solidarity, dating back to the days of the liberation struggle: "You gave us all the means with which we prosecuted our struggle and I say a good friend is one who stands by you when you are in trouble," he told Liu Zhufeng, the assistant minister for Construction, who visited Harare with a 13 strong delegation of Chinese businesspeople in March 2007.

A few days earlier, the US and Britain had condemned police attacks on the opposition which had left MDC leader Morgan Tsvangirai with a gash across the head and a severely swollen face. In Mugabe's view, Zimbabwe was "being faced by a struggle against great powers," and China was its ally.

The government-run *Herald* attempted to conjure past glories in an August 2007 story, which explained how Josiah Tongogara and eleven other liberation leaders attended Nanking Academy in 1966 to learn "mass mobilisation, military intelligence, political science, mass media, guerrilla war strategies and tactics." The newspaper even reprinted in ChiShona a version of Mao Zedong's famous aphorism about guerrillas being the fish who swim in the sea of the peasantry: "Simba rehove riri mumvura".

To the Chinese, the days when Comrade Li trained guerrillas from the Zimbabwe African National Liberation Army (ZANLA) in Tanzania are ancient history.

Chinese officials frequently reassure African leaders that they are "all weather friends". They cite the longstanding ties between Zimbabwe and China as a reason for continued good relations. But this is not the same as sharing nostalgia for an ideology which has long since gone out of fashion. As Beijing prepares for the 2008 Olympics and the government considers how to manage annual economic growth of 10%, few Chinese are still quoting Mao.

In the 1960s and 70s, China's primary interest in Africa was as a proxy to confront western powers, and later to curb the influence of the Soviet Union. Its support for ZANLA was partly to counter Soviet backing for Joshua Nkomo's Zimbabwe People's Revolutionary Army (ZIPRA).

Business comes first

Today, Beijing's interests are commercial and diplomatic.

"It's quite easy for Chinese to become rich in Zimbabwe," said Wu Jiangtao, dubbed "the most successful Chinese businessman in Zimbabwe" by the official news agency, Xinhua, in January 2007. The following month, *China Business News* reported on the relative merits of starting factories manufacturing furniture, glass and steel parts in Zimbabwe. Wang Wenming, described as "a former business diplomat to Africa", told of a Chinese garment factory which recovered its initial investment in the first year of operations.

The Chinese are in Africa for business, raw materials and to shore up African support for the Chinese claim on Taiwan and other matters of concern to Beijing at the United Nations. They do not intervene if a state abuses human rights, but nor do they like instability and conflict which may interfere with the viability of their investments.

For all these reasons, Zimbabwe is important only inasmuch as it may assist the

Chinese project. Despite the rhetoric of support for the government carried in the *People's Daily* and other official media, the Chinese are not blind to Zimbabwe's problems. "Zimbabwe is a much-discussed problem. Everyone realises there is a problem there. It is a sad situation," Zhou Yuxiao, Chinese ambassador in Harare, told the *Financial Times* in April 2007.

"The Zimbabwean people seem to be closer and closer to the edge of tolerance," said a Shanghai newspaper in mid-2006. "Although the national security police are everywhere, the people can't help complaining in public. No-one has a good word for the current government."

In similar vein, Xinhua reported in May 2007 on the reactions of Qi Feng and Wu Binbin, Chinese volunteer sports teachers, who were shocked to find there was no dormitory at Churchill Middle School in Harare. They had to bed down on mattresses in an office. Power cuts meant they spent long evenings talking to students in the dark. "We have experienced much hardship," said Qi.

When the government in Harare imposed price controls in mid-2007 in a desperate attempt to curb inflation, Chinese businessman Huang Xingang was given the choice of a five million Zim dollar fine or 30 days in prison for failing to display prices in his shop, Hubei Enterprises. Such incidents are likely to have far more impact on Chinese attitudes to the government in Harare than any residual loyalty to ZANU-PF.

A fickle friendship

The Chinese – like all outside powers in Africa – have a long history of changing sides when convenient.

In Angola, Beijing initially supported both the Popular Movement for the Liberation of Angola (MPLA) and the National Union for the Total Independence of Angola (UNITA) against the Portuguese colonialists. When the MPLA appealed for Soviet help in the mid-70s – just as Portuguese rule was coming to an end – the Chinese switched their support to a third group, the National Front for the Liberation of Angola (FNLA), based in Zaïre. Beijing armed both UNITA and the FNLA during a prolonged civil war from which they emerged the losers. Thirty years on, with the MPLA firmly in government, resource-rich Angola has become China's biggest trading partner in Africa and its second largest oil supplier after Saudi Arabia. So much for old loyalties.

All of which is likely to be good news for a post-Mugabe Zimbabwe.

Among Zimbabweans, resentment against China is widespread. Chinese traders selling cheap goods, widely derided as "Zhing Zhongs", have replaced indigenous businesses wiped out by "Operation *Murambatsvina*", the clearance programme which destroyed urban homes and shops in 2005. There are stories of buses from First Automobile Works, a Chinese company, which have never left their garage and of Chinese planes which Air Zimbabwe has never flown. Opposition parties are angry because the Chinese provided the technology which jams SW Radio Africa, a donor-funded radio station based in the UK which offers an alternative to the Zimbabwe Broadcasting Corporation. Most significantly, China has provided military aircraft and other weaponry – allegedly in return for stakes in platinum mining.

But resentment and anger will not help to revive the economy. While Zimbabwe has descended into nightmare, the world outside has changed. The West continued its long-term retreat, while China started to penetrate Africa. Managing Chinese investment and interests is one of the biggest challenges facing African governments in the first part of the 21st century, and a post-Mugabe Zimbabwe will be no exception.

China lends four times more money to Africa than the World Bank. Since 2000, trade between China and Africa has quintupled, reaching US$55 billion in 2006. Xinhua estimated that 750,000 Chinese were living in Africa by early 2007. No exact figure exists for Chinese direct investment in the continent but estimates vary between US$1.25 billion and US$6 billion. With the exception of South Africa, China's top ten trading partners in Africa are all oil producers. But Chinese prospectors are also combing the continent for copper, cobalt, platinum and other minerals and metals.

A strategy for Harare

Beijing has a well worked out policy towards Africa. The reverse is less true. Fragmented, often ill-governed Africa with its different, sometimes competing, states has no coherent policy towards China. When a new government in Harare begins to figure out its priorities, it will need to develop a pragmatic stance – preferably in concert with South Africa.

Consider the visit to Harare of a construction delegation from China in March 2007. Mugabe wanted Chinese companies to build rural homes, on the grounds that he sees rural Zimbabweans as showing "more loyalty than the urban people". In contrast, a new government in Harare is likely to want a rapid programme of urban regeneration to help those still destitute after "Operation *Murambatsvina*". Chinese companies might be the best placed to bid for contracts to build low-cost housing and their prices often undercut their western competitors. State construction companies from China are in a position to bundle these contracts with loans or barter deals. This could be exactly what Zimbabwe needs.

Across Africa, Chinese companies are building roads, bridges and other infrastructure – sometimes with funding from the World Bank. Some of these companies are accused of employing Chinese labour instead of hiring local Africans, but the costs of Chinese expatriate managers and engineers are far lower than their western counterparts. They also have a reputation for efficiency, often finishing projects ahead of schedule. Zimbabwe needs to rehabilitate its infrastructure and the Chinese could be the right people to help.

According to John Nkomo, parliamentary speaker, by mid-2007 China was the biggest foreign investor in Zimbabwe with interests to the value of US$600 million spanning 35 Chinese companies. Much of the sharply reduced commercial tobacco crop went to China in barter deals. With a new land policy, commercial farming may recover but it is unlikely to return to its previous dominant position in the Zimbabwean economy. A new government will have to encourage new sectors.

"China has offered Africa a new model that focuses on straight commercial relations and fair market prices without the ideological agenda," South African businessman Moeletsi Mbeki told the *New York Times* in November 2006. "They are not the first big foreign power to come to Africa, but they may be the first not to act as though they are some kind of patron or teacher or conqueror." This new relationship with foreign companies will be no longer colonial but a modern exchange – willing buyer, willing seller.

Natural resources are an obvious way to start. Zimbabwe has the world's second largest reserves of platinum; China is the world's largest buyer. That puts Harare in a position to strike a deal in return for long-term concessions but a new government must adopt a tough stance. Chinese investors and diplomats negotiate down to the wire. In response, a new government should hold out for decent minimum labour standards, a ban on the use of imported unskilled labour and reasonable tax revenue. The Chinese will threaten to go elsewhere, but they will be reluctant to forsake Zimbabwe's mineral reserves.

Past dealings between Harare and the Chinese have not been transparent. A new finance minister might find hidden clauses in contracts or no contracts at all. As reserves of foreign exchange have dwindled, bills for aircraft, engineering work and construction allegedly have been converted into loans. A new government, which found itself severely indebted to Beijing, could attempt to renegotiate repayment schedules, or choose to honour some of the barter arrangements which the current government has favoured.

After Mugabe, huge amounts of foreign aid will be promised by foreign donors. The most helpful response from western governments would be to cooperate with the Chinese in any recovery plan: "If there is a donors' conference or other aid effort for Zimbabwe, it would be important to involve the Chinese in a coordinated way," said Adrian Davis, head of the UK Department for International Development in Beijing.

Corruption will be the biggest factor working against Zimbabwean national interests in negotiations with the Chinese. Investors from China have no compunction about bribing to secure a deal which works for them. Zimbabweans involved in such negotiations will be a soft target if the individuals taking decisions are persuaded to back down by inducements. Whatever Mugabe may claim, it is delusion to pretend that Chinese investment is any sort of charitable project.

Lindsey Hilsum *is Beijing correspondent for Channel 4 News. Additional research by Kuang Ling.*

Dizzy worms and other disasters

From Amin to Mobutu, outside efforts to oust Africa's dictators are no guarantee of a better tomorrow. **Michael Holman** *considers the dubious precedents for foreign intervention in African crises.*

As dictatorial regimes approach the end of their life, look out for the "dizzy worm" syndrome. This malaise was most destructive in the former Zaïre, when the late President Mobutu Sese Seko announced cabinet reshuffles which left most observers as baffled about their significance as the country's unfortunate people. After one such reshuffle, a visiting journalist asked a western diplomat to explain what it all meant. The diplomat replied: "What do you get when you shake up a can of worms? Dizzy worms."

Mobutu kept up his dizzy worm strategy for years, shaking the political can. He was able to dupe well-meaning outsiders, to bewilder successive commentators, and to confuse political opponents, while the country he nominally ruled sank deeper into chaos.

By 1997, when South Africa tried to negotiate an elegant exit for Mobutu, it was far too late. There is no evidence that Pretoria's efforts made any impact – not even Nelson Mandela, then president, could work his magic. Instead it took cancer of the prostate and a hitherto unknown guerrilla movement, backed by Rwanda, to oust the man who ruled and plundered Zaire for nearly 30 years. Mobutu fled into exile, leaving behind a power vacuum that has contributed to the internal feuding and weak leadership in today's Democratic Republic of Congo (DRC).

There is surely a lesson for Zimbabwe here.

Robert Gabriel Mugabe is a very different creature from the late Mobutu Sese Seko, but both men have one thing in common. They have presided over the corruption of their country's political class, the police and armed forces. Able men and women have been transformed into an amoral and self-serving mafia, while senior politicians are reduced to mere onlookers in an unfolding tragedy which they lack the wisdom to resolve or the courage to confront. In short, most of Mr Mugabe's critics – within and without the ruling ZANU-PF party – have become "dizzy worms".

Few of the precedents for intervention in Africa offer any encouragement. Ironically, however, many of the leading participants in Zimbabwe's current crisis played important parts in one of the rare exceptions: Britain's re-engagement during the last weeks of the old Rhodesia.

The end of Rhodesia

In 1979, Britain despatched a governor, deployed troops, and supervised the elections from which independent Zimbabwe emerged – an example of successful external involvement in an African dispute.

The differences between Rhodesia in 1979 and Zimbabwe today illustrate the problems that face would-be mediators. These differences compound the dangers of external military intervention against Mugabe to a point where it is well nigh inconceivable:

- In 1979, Britain accepted its colonial responsibility and led international concern; today, no country plays this role.
- Zimbabwe's guerrilla-backed nationalist leadership was recognised world-wide; today the opposition is weak and unarmed.
- The constitutional settlement brokered in London in 1979 followed a debilitating civil war; today, those with access to scarce resources benefit materially from the economic crisis.
- The London talks took place with the consent and co-operation of all parties; today, the upper echelons of Zanu-PF are equivocal about participation.
- In 1979, the Commonwealth hosted a critical summit in Lusaka to pave the way for the London talks; today, the organisation stands mutely on the sidelines.

Almost three decades after Zimbabwe's independence, British military ambitions are limited instead to a contingency plan for the safe evacuation of up to 30,000 UK passport holders. In the event that this difficult but limited task were achieved, it would be hard to envisage any continuing UK military presence in Zimbabwe. British troops have enough to do in Iraq and Afghanistan.

A palace coup

Arguably, a more plausible scenario for external intervention would entail an invitation from a credible alliance of rebellious Zimbabwe ministers and opposition leaders. Then, and only then, a coalition of concerned parties led by South Africa might come to the country's aid. But there is little indication that ZANU-PF heavyweights – the "dizzy worms" – would lend support to what would amount to a palace coup.

The most likely alternative is a gradual drift into deeper misery, with Robert Mugabe contesting elections in 2008 and the fate of the country vested firmly in the hands of ZANU-PF. No cavalry will ride to the rescue of a people worn down by poverty and malnutrition – for reasons which are both simple and compelling.

Military intervention in Africa's crises has proved a hazardous experience. Tanzania's role in the overthrow of Uganda's dictator, Idi Amin, brought only short-term success. United States' intervention in Somalia in 1993 exacerbated internal feuds. Other approaches – from personal mediation to the deployment of UN peacekeepers – have had mixed results or are clearly inappropriate for Zimbabwe.

Uganda
Tanzania's intervention in Uganda in 1979 provides the nearest parallel to Zimbabwe today – and also the starkest warning.

One of Amin's first acts, almost as devastating for the Ugandan economy as Mugabe's land grab has been for Zimbabwe, was the expulsion of the country's Asian community. Wanton killings and systematic torture became commonplace, until Idi Amin went a step too far, sending a small contingent of Ugandan troops to "invade" neighbouring Tanzania. The incursion was the pretext for which President Julius Nyerere had waited. The Tanzanian army crossed into Uganda, flanked by a band of Ugandan guerrillas.

Within weeks, Amin was in exile. But his brutal tyranny did not give way to democracy. Rigged elections in 1980 restored former prime minister, Milton Obote, to power. Obote, a close friend of Nyerere who had provided him with a home in Dar es Salaam during his years in exile, introduced a new reign of terror. Only when guerrillas loyal to Yoweri Museveni overthrew the Obote regime in 1986 did stability return to Uganda. Some years later, Mr Museveni is still president and opposition parties are discouraged. The president's critics and would-be successors need to act with care.

The usefulness of more recent instances of external intervention is more debateable.

Sierra Leone, Congo

Britain's military intervention in Sierra Leone in 2000 began ostensibly as an operation to secure the country's airport and evacuate foreign nationals. The short-term outcome was the restoration of stability in a land where rag-tag bands of fighters had terrorised the local population. These gangs were no match for well-armed professionals but the prospects for economic and social recovery remain distant.

South African president, Thabo Mbeki, would probably claim that his efforts to play the conciliator in Cote d'Ivoire and in the Great Lakes have born fruit. He can point to his role in the DRC, when in 2002 he virtually confined delegates from rival militias to their hotel rooms in South Africa's Sun City until they emerged with a peace deal. The exercise paved the way to Congo's elections, but the peace requires the presence of 17,000 UN soldiers to maintain it.

Angola, Mozambique

In Angola, UN peacekeeping efforts initially failed to overcome the enmity between the rebel UNITA movement and the ruling MPLA. Not until UNITA leader Jonas Savimbi was killed in battle did the conflict end.

In Mozambique, it took the quiet persistence of church groups to mediate between the ruling Frelimo and the rebel Renamo and lay the foundation for an end to the fighting.

While these examples show that in certain instances mediation can assist, they also suggest that there is a grim hurdle that must first be crossed: all these countries had undergone a civil war, tantamount to a brutal softening-up of the protagonists that prepared the ground for external conciliators.

Of course there are other methods of applying pressure from outside, short of sending in troops. But the record of economic sanctions against Rhodesia and South Africa is mixed. Few would attribute the end of white rule to sanctions alone.

Kenya

Those who maintain that an economic squeeze will bring the change they desire in Zimbabwe might recall the case of Kenya, where a decade of pressure from western donors on the government of Daniel arap Moi brought little result.

In the late 1990s, aid donors imposed a freeze on assistance to the corrupt and autocratic government of President Daniel arap Moi, in an effort to bring about a multi-party democracy and clean government. Moi eventually conceded, lifting a ban on opposition parties. Some donors saw this as a considerable achievement.

Others were sceptical. Far from setting Kenya on the path to genuine multi-party politics, they argued, donor pressure had forced him to modernise his one-party rule. The reforms he reluctantly adopted created safety-valves for dissent, thus effectively extending his time in office.

A decade later, Moi's successor, President Mwai Kibaki has turned out to be marginally better than his predecessors, but the corruption that was endemic under Moi continues under Kibaki and the vast goodwill which greeted his victory in the December 2003 elections has been squandered.

However, an earlier experience in Kenya, also a British colony, is relevant to Zimbabwe. At independence, one thousand white farmers occupied the best farmlands – a relatively small number, compared to the five thousand who once lived in Zimbabwe. But Britain, backed by West Germany and the World Bank, was significantly more generous when it came to supporting a land redistribution programme. The foreign funds provided for land redistribution in Kenya were double the value, in real terms, of those made available to Zimbabwe twenty years later.

Thabo Mbeki and regional mediation
The key player in any lasting solution to Zimbabwe's crisis will surely be President Thabo Mbeki. Often cast as the villain by the western press, theories for his failure to confront his neighbour abound: some critics say that he is overawed by the older man; or that he is a secret sympathiser; or that he has an abiding loyalty to a former comrade in arms.

Much of this is speculation, but the last theory is plain nonsense. Mbeki is akin to ANC royalty and knows his party's history. ANC guerrillas worked closely with the Zimbabwe African People's Union (ZAPU) led by Joshua Nkomo, Mugabe's arch rival. Both organisations shared Soviet Russia as their main patron. Relations between ZANU-PF and ANC fighters, on the other hand, were so strained that on more than one occasion they clashed on Zimbabwean soil.

Could President Mbeki have taken a tougher stance? Certainly. Could he have changed the tone of African efforts to press for reform in Zimbabwe? Most observers agree that he could have done. Would it have made any difference? Probably not.

> ### "Advocates of a 'Switch off the lights' tactic assume Mugabe would respond rationally. On recent evidence, this is unlikely."

Mbeki's critics contend that he should apply pressure on Mugabe in the same way that the Pretoria government forced Rhodesian prime minister, Ian Douglas Smith, to negotiate in 1979, by restricting supplies of fuel and electricity from South Africa. Notwithstanding the important differences between Rhodesia then and Zimbabwe today, advocates of this "Switch Off The Lights" tactic assume that Mugabe would respond rationally. The recent evidence, however, suggests this is unlikely. Mugabe appears prepared to die in his metaphorical bunker.

Waiting in the wings: Angola
Far from prompting Mugabe's hasty departure, a more likely possibility is that the government of Zimbabwe could appeal for support from its neighbours. Only one country in the region might come to his aid, but one would be enough for Mugabe: The Angolan government of José Eduardo dos Santos has military resources and the revenue from oil to fund such a venture – and Dos Santos is known to be sympathetic to Mugabe.

The likely reaction was tested in early 2007, in what may well have been a kite-flying exercise. Media reports that Angola was preparing to send 3,000 paramilitary police on a "training exercise" to Harare were subsequently denied, but the incident was a timely reminder to opponents of the Zimbabwean military that Angolan troops could yet be waiting on the sidelines.

Aid
If *intervention* under current circumstances is all but inconceivable, and *invitation* is unlikely to be forthcoming, external actors must reconsider their strategy for

Zimbabwe. Perhaps the greatest single irony is that food from the West, distributed by the UN World Food Programme (WFP), has sustained Zimbabwe's crisis.

In November 2001, government evictions of white farmers combined with severe drought to leave half a million Zimbabweans at risk of starvation. The WFP stepped in to provide food aid, largely without consulting the governments that bear the cost. No conditions were attached, leading to the current absurdity of a situation where the consequences of the land grab have been alleviated by donors. Their humanitarian purpose sustains a corrupt regime, just as a decade of food aid to Sudan prolonged its civil war by cushioning rival leaders from the full impact of their conflict.

Commercial institutions are also implicated in the battle for democracy – and not for the first time in Africa. In 2006, London-based Standard Chartered bank provided an $80m line of credit to Zimbabwe. This contrasts with the international opprobrium targeted at South Africa's apartheid regime in the mid-1980s, when foreign banks refused to underwrite Pretoria's sovereign debt. Soon after, Barclays pulled out of South Africa, prompted by a student-led boycott in Britain that had begun to dent its profits and harm its profile.

It is time to seek greater transparency about the role of international institutions, whether humanitarian or commercial, in Zimbabwe. Aid agencies should disclose the amount of food aid provided to the country and negotiate the conditions on which it is supplied with donor governments. The role of international banks in Zimbabwe needs to be monitored, their loans investigated – and, if necessary, named and shamed.

Michael Holman *was brought up in Rhodesia and now lives in London. He was Africa editor of the* Financial Times *1984-2002. His first novel,* Last Orders at Harrods, *was re-published by Abacus in March this year. The sequel,* Fatboy and the Dancing Ladies, *was published in June 2007 and he is currently working on the third.*

Not being Nelson Mandela

Zimbabwe's opposition movement has enjoyed sponsorship and acclaim from sympathisers abroad. **Robert I. Rotberg** *argues that the Movement for Democratic Change would follow the precedents for popular leadership in Africa.*

Nelson Mandela emerged from prison in 1990 to demonstrate the best practices of democratic African leadership. His inclusive and participatory values matched those that had been affirmed for decades in neighbouring Botswana under Presidents Seretse Khama and Ketumile Masire. Khama's example had been the lodestar of democratic leadership in Africa: the sure manner in which he had articulated a clear vision for his country and the straightforward way in which he had mobilised the people of Botswana in support of democratic values were exemplary. Mandela and Khama (followed by Masire and now, in Botswana, by President Festus Mogae) suggest the power of individual agency for good. Effective, popular leadership can flourish in Africa.

President Robert Mugabe is today's African poster child for damaging, venal leadership. Zimbabwe's once high levels of good governance have been driven into the ground; political freedoms have been universally denied; and even ZANU-PF has come to chafe under the exactions and Duvalier-like capriciousness of a Pol Pot style ruler. Under Mugabe, Zimbabweans have become more immiserated than ever before.

Worst of all, as I write, no uprising of the downtrodden masses, no purple or rose revolutions, and no alliances between opposition politicians and soldiers and police appeared promising. Powerful neighbours were not going to intervene, as Tanzania had done so successfully in Idi Amin's Uganda and as others had done so well in Mobutu Sese Seko's Zaïre.

South Africa has always refused to follow their lead, often defending Mugabe's excesses within and outside the African Union. External sanctions, even the American "smart sanctions", have accomplished little. Despite the internal chaos and near-universal condemnation from non-Africans and the United Nations, no one can foresee precisely how this mayhem would be curtailed.

Fortunately, abundant good leaders and positive leadership are available for the post-Mugabe, post ZANU-PF era. Within the principal MDC grouping, still run by Tsvangirai, are a number of persons capable of leading a free Zimbabwe back to liberty and prosperity.

No Somali-type end-game is lurking on the horizon, despite the horrendous destruction already wreaked. The intrinsic high levels of education among Zimbabweans, and the Zimbabwe people's resilient political culture, predict a better outcome in a restored state. Tsvangirai has in effect won several popular elections already. He has demonstrated integrity and a strong ability to lead; he has articulated excellent ideas about how best to reform Zimbabwe; and his associates and collaborators in the MDC are also capable.

The remnants of ZANU-PF, particularly the jousting wannabe heirs to Mugabe – such as Emmerson Mnangagwa, defeated MP for Kwekwe, former cabinet minister and speaker of parliament, and Solomon Mujuru, former army commander and cabinet member – have all enriched themselves since Mugabe unleashed the forces of wild corruption in the 1990s. What Zimbabwe needs are leaders like Tsvangirai who have not helped destroy their country, preyed on its people or consorted with evil. Mugabe's successors must work for the people, not against them.

Extracted from an article first published in the *Mail & Guardian,* April 26th 2007, and edited for clarity.

Sleights of hand at Lancaster House

Promises of international funding for land reform were deliberately forgotten, recalls **Shridath 'Sonny' Ramphal,** *secretary-general of the Commonwealth from 1975 to 1990.* He told **Gugulethu Moyo** *and* **Mark Ashurst** *about his role as an advisor to Robert Mugabe and Joshua Nkomo, leaders of the Patriotic Front of independence movements in Rhodesia, during constitutional negotiations at Lancaster House, London in 1979.*

SSR: I think Zimbabwe today comes out of Zimbabwe of yesterday. Yes I do, because I think there is no one factor that can explain what is going on in Zimbabwe. I think you have to go back to the beginning to a statistic that never left my mind from the moment I heard it and that is that in Rhodesia 80% of the arable land was owned and occupied by less than 5% of the population. That statistic colours everything that happened in the process that led to Lancaster House.

It was about land in the beginning; it was about land during the struggle; it has remained about land today. The land issue in Rhodesia / Zimbabwe is not ancient history. It is modern history. Black Zimbabweans were dispossessed of the land that was theirs within the lifetime memory of some, and certainly in the lifetime of the generation before. Now, if you forget that, then you can't answer rationally any of the pertinent questions about Zimbabwe. And I think it is the forgetting of that that ultimately has led us to where we are.

Who has done the forgetting?
Well, many people – including, I fear, the government of Zimbabwe, post-independence. But that fault, that forgetting, has to be set in a context which explains how it came to happen. My own feeling is that we came very close to getting Zimbabwe right at the Lancaster House Conference.

Is "forgetting" the right word? Has there been perhaps a wilful amnesia or was there some other kind of agreement to put this, the redistribution issue, the land issue, to one side?
Well, yes. I think the first ten years, what was in effect a moratorium on land redistribution in which the government seem to have concurred, was part of the forgetting.

Was there an agreement to forget do you think?
There was an agreement to put it to one side, to defer, which is almost inexplicable. People struggled to repossess their patrimony and the stage was set for that to happen, and you decide that you will wait for 10 years before justice is done. Of course in those 10 years all kinds of other priorities began to intrude so that the land issue, which should have been solved in the beginning, was put on the back burner and a kind of honeymoon period was enjoyed between the new government and those who were on the land. The government of Zimbabwe was very popular in those first ten years.

You say that this amnesia, or the setting to one side, is almost inexplicable. Did it seem inexplicable to you at the time?
It always did. I thought the situation could only get worse. I had not realised that the dispossessed in Zimbabwe would be so long-suffering, but I had to bow to the reality – they were.

Going back to Lancaster House, was land the only question on which the parties didn't agree? Were there any other concerns in that draft constitution?
It was the major stumbling block. And it came up very early. While the Patriotic Front was absolutely clear that the land issue was central, the draft constitution contained the standard convention clause on property, which was a guarantee against the deprivation of property without the payment of prompt and adequate compensation. It was what was in the tenets of international governance, in the UN conventions, but what it signalled to Mugabe and Nkomo was maintaining the status quo on land.

Now there are reasons that explain it and if Lord Carrington was sitting here he would tell you, no doubt, that he wasn't negotiating only with Mugabe and Nkomo, he was negotiating with Smith, he was negotiating with General Walls, and there was no way he was going to get a constitution through which didn't guarantee the status quo on land. But he was faced with the very opposite requirement from the Patriotic Front, and after all they represented the vast majority of the people of Zimbabwe.

There was something of a sleight of hand because when Mugabe and Nkomo threatened to leave Lancaster House unless the land issue was dealt with in a way which would allow for land redistribution, the fudge was: "You will be helped to pay the compensation that the constitution requires to be paid." It was such a standard provision, but it was not a provision designed to deal with historical wrongs. So if you had to have the provision, then you had to have resources to pay the compensation for land acquired.

How do you recall the personalities that were involved?

I was very close to Robert Mugabe and Joshua Nkomo. I really didn't see anything of Ian Smith and General Walls or even Bishop Muzorewa. They kept their distance, they had their own advisors. They were working against everything the Commonwealth was working for. But we did see Mugabe and Nkomo every day, they were at the conference in the day and with the Commonwealth Secretariat in the evening.

What was the chemistry like between Mugabe and Nkomo?

Quite good. They presented a united front. We all knew that ZAPU and ZANU were different political parties. Those differences were not hidden but they were united on a bigger cause.

Can you confirm whether at one point there was just you, Lord Carrington, Joshua Nkomo and Robert Mugabe in one room where you tried to find a way through this impasse over land and compensations. Is that correct?

No. There was a meeting in my home, in the secretariat residence, between myself and Mugabe and Nkomo. That was the moment when the conference could have broken up. They had walked out, they had said they could not subscribe to a constitution which meant that there could not be land distribution.

Carrington's plan as chairman of the conference was that we must have agreement on the draft constitution, which included this provision. He said to the Patriotic Front: "If you do not agree to the provisions of the draft constitution, but other delegations do, the conference will resume without you". In other words, Lancaster House would be reduced to the British government and Bishop Muzorewa [prime minister in the pre-election, biracial government], Ian Smith and General Walls. That was almost unthinkable.

The frontline states let it be known to the British government that there was no way they would accept that. Bear in mind that Lancaster House was made possible by a Commonwealth deal at the heads of government meeting in Lusaka. So the support of Zambian president, Kenneth Kaunda and Tanzanian president, Julius Nyerere, in particular, but also Botswana and others, for the whole process was terribly important.

It was in that situation that I talked with Nkomo and Mugabe. I said: "First of all, you cannot let Lancaster House break up, or worse still, end without you. Secondly, you are not going to be on good ground if the reason for the break-up is attributed to your refusal to have a clause protecting private property in the constitution of Zimbabwe. This is a clause that is in every constitution. So we have to find another way."

I made the suggestion that we must find a way to get a guarantee of support from the British government, internationally, of funds that would allow them to compulsorily acquire enough land to begin the process of land resettlement. And I said to them: "I'm going to discuss this with the American ambassador, Kingman Brewster, and I will come back to you." I invited the American ambassador to meet with me. I said to him: "If you don't help now Lancaster House will break up: all that we have achieved will be lost and that will only strengthen the hand of apartheid South Africa." Kingman said: "I am with you, I think this is the right approach. I have to talk to Washington. Give me 24 hours."

He came back the next day. He had spoken to Cyrus Vance who had spoken to President Carter and they had authorised Brewster to say to me, and through me to the Patriotic Front, that they would support the establishment of an agricultural development fund and they would make a substantial contribution to it; that they would recognise the right of the government after the elections to use this fund to help to defray any compensation that had to be paid under the constitution; that the fund would be a responsibility they would accept, providing it was matched by the British government and had an international character. That was the American response. It could not have been more positive.

Can you indicate a scale of the contribution?
He left me with no doubt that it would be very substantial.

I said: "That's fine you telling me, but you have to say this to the Patriotic Front." The next day, the deputy ambassador came to my home and met Dr Mugabe and Dr Nkomo and told them what the ambassador had told me. He confirmed to them that this was the position of the American government and that they would inform the British government. He recommended that on that basis the Patriotic Front should return to the conference.

It didn't just end there. The frontline states were putting a great deal of pressure on the British government. Then the Patriotic Front drew up a statement, on the basis of which they would go back into the conference, recording the assurances that they had received.

They met with the Foreign Office the night before returning to the conference and showed them the statement that Dr Nkomo would read out the next morning when the conference resumed. Then they distributed the statement to the members of the Southern Africa Committee because they wanted there to be no doubt whatever, in anybody's mind, that this was the basis on which they were going back.

It sounds a rather easy assurance to give: that there would be an unspecified sum of money to support things like redistribution and development. Given how vexed and difficult those issues had been up until that point, wouldn't you have expected a bit more detail?
No, I don't think so. You are dealing with the government of the United States, the government of Britain. Solid assurances were recorded in the documents of the conference and notified to all Commonwealth countries. It wasn't a little thing.

It didn't specify a sum, but specifying a sum would have been very difficult in the context of Zimbabwe. What farms? How many of them? What cost?

Was there any mention of a contribution from the government of Zimbabwe at a future date?
No, no. That would have been strange.

We know from the Foreign Office Minutes that they were having those discussions themselves though.
They may well have been having discussions not with the Patriotic Front but later on with the Mugabe government. Indeed, later on they obviously did have discussions with the new government because it was out of those discussions that came the decision to defer. But they would have been outside the conference; not just outside the conference but post-independence.

So at the time, you were confident that you had obtained the guarantees that were necessary to satisfy everybody?
I was. And I think the Patriotic Front was.

So how does one now go about calculating the responsibilities of outsiders towards trying to resolve the matter?
I don't know that you can calculate in that way. You would first have to get a ball-park figure and it would probably now have to be a situation in which the government of Zimbabwe itself played a role. You know we are nearly 30 years from Lancaster House.

In all this I have been talking about governments, about the leaders of the Patriotic Front. But the people of Zimbabwe are basically what all this was about and I have a deep consciousness of the terrible plight of those people. I'm not on the Commonwealth scene now but I believe the Commonwealth has an ongoing responsibility to those people. Forget leaders and all that: it is a terrible human disaster in Zimbabwe.

The Commonwealth cannot ever relinquish responsibility to those people. It was like Oliver Tambo telling me that black people of South Africa never left the Commonwealth. The Commonwealth must take the position that it never left the people of Zimbabwe.

'We have now obtained assurances'

This statement was released by **Joshua Nkomo** *on behalf of the Patriotic Front of Zimbabwean independence movements on October 18th 1979. The statement followed a meeting the previous evening between Nkomo, Mugabe and the British Foreign Office and a private meeting with Lord Carrington, chairman of the constitutional negotiations at Lancaster House.*

"When the conference adjourned we stated that we required clarification on the fund relating to the land question to which the Chairman had made reference.

We have now obtained assurances that depending on the successful outcome of the Conference, Britain, the United States of America and other countries will participate in a multinational financial donor effort to assist in land, agricultural and economic development programmes.

These assurances go a long way in allaying the great concern we have over the whole land question, arising from the great need our people have for land and our commitment to satisfying that need when in government.

In these circumstances, and in clarification of our statement of the 11th of October 1979, we are now able to say that if we are satisfied beyond doubt about the vital issues of the transitional arrangements, there will not be need to revert to discussion on the constitution, including those issues on which we reserved our position."

From the personal archive of Sir Shridath 'Sonny' Ramphal.

Grasping the nettle

The Commonwealth has lost the influence gained during Africa's independence struggles, writes **Derek Ingram.** *A renewed effort to engage with Zimbabwe is long overdue and a test of credibility.*

Zimbabwe is a Commonwealth problem. The fact that it is not at the moment a member of the Commonwealth should be disregarded. Its crisis has seriously affected most Commonwealth member countries in Africa and others beyond, notably the UK. Commonwealth concerns have never been restricted to the affairs of member countries.

In a previous incarnation, as Southern Rhodesia and a part of the short-lived Central African Federation, the country has haunted the Commonwealth since 1922 when a handful of whites voted to become a "self-governing colony" rather than join South Africa. No other region has taken up so much of the Commonwealth's time and energy.

The Harare Declaration of Commonwealth Principles, a much-admired statement of ambitions for the modern world, was the product of a Commonwealth Heads of Government Meeting (CHOGM) hosted in 1991 by President Robert Mugabe. But since Zimbabwe walked out of the organisation, pre-empting its likely expulsion at the end of the Abuja CHOGM in 2003, the country appears to have been written out of this historic script. No mention of Zimbabwe appears in the Minutes of the 2005 CHOGM in Malta – nor, incredibly, in the 2005 biennial report of the Commonwealth secretary-general.

This is all totally at odds with the precedent set by the withdrawal of apartheid South Africa from the Commonwealth in 1961. John Diefenbaker, prime minister of Canada, argued then that South Africa could not be a member so long as it was an apartheid state. But he insisted there should be "always be a candle in the window" to await the country's return to the fold when apartheid was gone. There was.

The official Commonwealth position on South Africa was always that its quarrel was not with the country's people but its government. Oliver Tambo, president of the African National Congress, famously said that South Africa had never left the Commonwealth because its people had never been asked. So it is now with Zimbabwe.

The Commonwealth has played an important role in Africa's independence. Over many years leading up to the end of apartheid in 1994, the Commonwealth trained South African exiles to become public servants, teachers and technicians in preparation for the day when their country became democratic. The foreign ministry staff and diplomatic service of Namibia (formerly Southwest Africa, and never part of the Empire or Commonwealth before independence) were almost wholly trained in Commonwealth countries.

Commonwealth officials were midwives at the birth of the new Zimbabwe in 1980, overseeing the end of the liberation war and the elections that immediately followed. Julius Nyerere, Malcolm Fraser, Kenneth Kaunda, Michael Manley and – yes – Margaret Thatcher were the pre-eminent Commonwealth players.

Diary of a separation
Relations with Zimbabwe soured in the first days of Secretary-General Don McKinnon's tenure. The two have barely exchanged words since 2000 when, immediately after taking office, McKinnon flew to Harare to see Zimbabwe's president. He was kept waiting for three days before a stormy encounter.

The CHOGM of 2002 was held in Coolum, Australia, days before the March presidential elections in Zimbabwe. Mugabe did not attend, but sent Stan Mudenge, his foreign minister. The gathered heads of state issued a statement warning that if the Commonwealth Observer Group disputed the election result, Zimbabwe could be suspended from membership.

A so-called troika of leaders – Presidents Thabo Mbeki of South Africa, Olusegun Obasanjo of Abuja and Prime Minister John Howard of Australia – was set up to decide what action might be taken by the Commonwealth after the election. They met in London, after the Observer Group's critical report on the election, and decided that Zimbabwe must be suspended.

Fatally, the troika agreed to meet again to review the situation. Mbeki had been hesitant all along about the suspension and the three leaders soon fell out over how to handle Zimbabwe. The troika, convened to respond in the immediate situation of the election period, collapsed into acrimony. The dispute might have been less acute if the problem had been delegated instead to the Commonwealth Ministerial Action

Group, a more representative body of eight foreign ministers which exists primarily to deal with such diplomatic quandaries.

> *"It was in Lusaka in 1979 that Commonwealth leaders worked out the plan to end the war in Rhodesia. Independence was celebrated within a year."*

Since the 2003 CHOGM in Abuja, the impression has been created that Zimbabwe is no longer the Commonwealth's business. Privately, officials from the Commonwealth Secretariat have tried many times to re-establish a dialogue with Harare. There have been unofficial contacts at international meetings but relations between Mbeki and McKinnon have long been cool and their differences are compounded by the apparently protective public attitude to the Mugabe regime assumed by the African Union and Southern Africa Development Community (SADC). Of the SADC's 14 members, 12 are in the Commonwealth.

Sensibilities were further aggravated in 2004, by the lifting of the suspension from membership of Pakistan, as a result of Western pressure. To African countries, this looks very much like a case of double standards. The Commonwealth seems to be treating Zimbabwe in a different way from Pakistan, which still has a military government and remains in serious breach of the organisation's democratic principles. Africans see it as a case of one law for Asia and another for Africa.

One step at a time
A first priority for the Commonwealth should be to try to mediate to restore a reasonable dialogue between London and Zimbabwe. The arrival, in July 2007, of a new British prime minister presents this opportunity, although such a move seems unlikely until a new Commonwealth secretary-general takes office in March 2008.

A second priority is to tackle the divisive question of whether any attempt should be made to secure Mugabe's retirement by offering him amnesty from prosecution. SADC leaders in their present mood will want Mugabe to be allowed to spend his last days in peace and comfort, and this is said to be part of the Mbeki proposals under discussion with representatives from ZANU-PF and the opposition Movement for Democratic Change (MDC).

For pragmatic reasons, amnesty from prosecution might appear a worthwhile price to alleviate massive suffering. However, it would be a terrible example to a world that has at last set up the legal infrastructure to punish criminal leaders – and Mugabe is not likely to believe that such promises would be kept.

Commonwealth leaders meeting in Uganda for their biennial summit in November 2007 must engage again with the situation in Zimbabwe. To ignore the subject any longer will seriously harm the Commonwealth's reputation. A scheduled gathering, known as The Retreat, is the place to do it – an opportunity for leaders to meet privately at Munyonyo resort on Lake Victoria, without officials and away from the main venue in Kampala.

The Retreat formula, now copied by other international bodies, was invented in 1973 by Canadian prime minister, Pierre Trudeau, to tackle just this kind of problem. Down the years it has served the Commonwealth well. It was at the Retreat in Lusaka in 1979 that Commonwealth leaders worked out the plan to end the war in Rhodesia. Independence was celebrated within a year.

The strong, long-established tradition of consensus, which operates at every Commonwealth gathering, augurs well for such a discussion. If three or four heads of government refuse to discuss Zimbabwe, even in the Retreat, the Commonwealth may once again find itself unable to act. However, tradition implies that unhappy heads should give way.

Once it has resolved to act, the Commonwealth must look to the future – beyond Mugabe – in order to help the Zimbabwean people prepare for the days when a new government is in place. A first step could be setting up a small working group with two urgent objectives:

1. To work out an immediate plan to assist Zimbabwean refugees, including training for Zimbabweans whose careers have been interrupted, and a crash programme to restore standards in health care and governance. This will contribute

to the restoration of an impartial public service and judiciary.

2. To provide support for the proper conduct of any election in Zimbabwe. Since 1980, the Commonwealth has gained huge experience of monitoring elections on all continents. That Zimbabwe is not a member should not, in theory, prevent the Commonwealth from sending election observers. Not least since re-admission to membership would hardly be possible without its *imprimatur*.

African leaders are all known privately to be deeply worried about Zimbabwe. However, until some dialogue is achieved with Harare, Mugabe is most unlikely to accept Commonwealth election observers. From its wealth of talent, the Commonwealth could – as a minimum first step – appoint eminent persons to guide and advise other observer missions. These must be on the ground early and remain there well after the election.

Derek Ingram *is a writer on Commonwealth affairs and vice-president of the Royal Commonwealth Society. He has covered every Commonwealth Heads of Government Meeting since 1969.*

A broadly held view?

Zimbabwe was suspended from the Commonwealth after the presidential election of 2002 and withdrew from the Commonwealth on December 7th 2003, pre-empting expulsion by the Commonwealth Heads of Government Meeting in Abuja, Nigeria. The incident triggered a deep rift among Commonwealth members, with some African leaders casting doubt on the usefulness of the institution. South African president **Thabo Mbeki** *blamed the Commonwealth chairman, Australian prime minister John Howard, for ignoring the views of African presidents in a troika of Commonwealth leaders tasked with assessing the situation in Zimbabwe.*

"When it met in Coolum, Australia in 2002, CHOGM charged a troika, made up of the chair of the Commonwealth, the prime minister of Australia and the presidents of Nigeria and South Africa, to take action on Zimbabwe in the event that the Commonwealth Elections Observer Team made a negative finding about the 2002 Zimbabwe Presidential elections ...

This Observer Team concluded that "the conditions in Zimbabwe did not adequately allow for a free expression of will by the electors." On this basis the troika decided to suspend Zimbabwe from the councils of the Commonwealth for one year, which should have meant the conclusion of its mandated mission.

However the troika also decided that it would meet again in a year's time to consider the evolution of the situation in Zimbabwe ... Later the then chair of the Commonwealth, Australian prime minister, John Howard, insisted that the troika should meet six months earlier than it had decided ...

The reason for this otherwise unscheduled meeting was that he wanted the troika to impose additional sanctions on Zimbabwe, for which it had no mandate. The two other members of the troika told him as much and argued that the troika should meet at the end of the one-year, as originally agreed ...

Accordingly, contrary to all normal practice, the chair decided to announce to the world at a press conference, that he disagreed with his colleagues in the troika and wanted more Commonwealth sanctions imposed on Zimbabwe.

The majority on the troika then advised the chair that if he wanted additional sanctions, he, and not the troika, would have to get a mandate from all the heads of government of the Commonwealth. They also indicated their opposition to the continuation of the suspension beyond the one-year that had been agreed earlier. Nevertheless, the chair requested the secretary general to consult these heads.

In his report, after this process of consultation, the secretary general said: "Some member governments take the view that it is time to lift Zimbabwe's suspension from the councils of the Commonwealth when the one-year period expires on March 19th 2003. Some others feel that there is no justification for such a step and that there is in fact reason to impose stronger measures. However, the broadly held view is that heads of government wish to review matters at CHOGM in Nigeria in December 2003 and that the suspension of Zimbabwe should remain in place pending discussions on the matter at CHOGM."

Unfortunately, the secretary general has never explained what he meant by "the broadly held view", especially in the light of the fact that some heads of government were not consulted and others were wrongly led to believe that we supported the continuation of the suspension.

In its statement after the Abuja CHOGM, SADC and Uganda said: "We ... wish to express our displeasure and deep concern with the dismissive, intolerant and rigid attitude displayed by some members of the Commonwealth during the deliberations. The Commonwealth has always operated on the basis of consensus. We fear that this attitude is destined to undermine the spirit that makes the Commonwealth a unique family of nations."

Extracted from *Letter from the President*, ANC Today, Volume 3, No. 49, December 12-18th 2003, and edited for clarity.

5.TRANSITION

Process matters as much as substance

A new constitution is no panacea for Zimbabwe, writes **Gugulethu Moyo***. Principles are important for a democratic society, but a deal brokered behind closed doors will not solve the crisis of legitimacy.*

Questions about a new constitution are a recurring feature of debates about how to begin repairing the damage in Zimbabwe. At the heart of the current malaise lies the simple truth that Zimbabwe needs fundamental political change – a different contract between the government and the people. Constitutional reform will not, of itself, resolve the crisis. But it can help develop a set of principles around which to build a more cohesive society.

In September 2007, parliament ratified Constitutional Amendment 18 with support from both the ruling party and the opposition. MDC and ZANU-PF leaders explained that the cross-party deal, following negotiations mediated by South Africa, was a necessary compromise. The agreement has been interpreted as a sign that mediation by the Southern African Development Community (SADC) is succeeding.

Just days after details of Amendment 18 were announced, stories were leaked to the press that the bargain struck in Pretoria reached well beyond what had been made public.

However much a deal on the constitution may seem to the politicians to be necessary and inevitable, important constituencies back home are not convinced. Regardless of the substance, further constitutional arrangements made in closed negotiations without the participation of a broad spectrum of people will lack democratic legitimacy.

Proponents of constitutional reform who have not been party to recent negotiations have a different definition of success. The National Constitutional Assembly – a broad-based lobby group which includes church leaders, journalists, lawyers, academics and grassroots activists – have been largely consistent in their hopes and ambitions. Their most important demand is that reform should be a democratic process. They want an open, deliberative constitutional assembly in which popular participation essential.

In the wake of Amendment 18, a little perspective helps. Since 1999, the Movement for Democratic Change (MDC) and its allies in civil society – led by the National Constitutional Assembly – insisted that constitutional reform should not become the property of any party or group of parties. Zimbabwe needs a new people-driven constitution, framed through an inclusive and participatory process. For eight years, the MDC refused to condone any process dominated by the ruling party.

During that time, ZANU-PF and its hegemony have at least paid lip service to joining negotiations on anything and everything *except* the process of constitutional reform. On the critical issue of the constitution, the ruling party has not surrendered control. ZANU-PF is not ready to allow others to jeopardise a system carefully devised to legitimise and prolong its rule.

A wedge in the door
Regional leaders exerted pressure on politicians from both sides. No-one wanted to be seen to refuse to compromise in a process on which so much depends. Proponents of Amendment 18 argue that these reforms pushed a wedge into the door which, once opened, will lead ineluctably to further reform.

I find it hard to find grounds for this optimism. Concessions from the ruling party have been strictly limited to very narrow improvements in the electoral system. Amendment 18 has scarcely reduced the constitutionally privileged role of ZANU-PF.

The political process which will follow the constitutional revision has yet to run its course. It has been suggested that the two sides are hopeful they can devise a new constitution by the close of negotiations in October 2007. If these reports are correct, the participants are missing the point. A constitution should not be written in a few weeks by a handful of politicians at a conference table.

An enduring constitution requires the long ordeal of developing broad public consensus and building trust. Given the deep cleavages in society and the popular loss of trust in political institutions, it is unlikely that consensus can be achieved in a short period.

There are obvious parallels with the process which devised Zimbabwe's current constitution, brokered at Lancaster House in 1979. The independence document was as much the outcome of a peace process as an effort to draft fundamental legislation. Preoccupation with securing a ceasefire after a bloody civil war may have prevented a constitutional process more conducive to striking a balance between conflicting interests.

Then as now, those at the negotiating table were political leaders – all men – from rival factions: Prime Minister Abel Muzorewa; his deputy, Silas Mundawarara; Ian Smith, former prime minister of the Rhodesian government; Robert Mugabe and Joshua Nkomo, for the Patriotic Front. The British government, represented by Lord Carrington, played a dominant role as mediator. No other groups were represented.

At the start of the Lancaster House talks, Lord Carrington made clear that he wanted to settle the constitutional questions quickly before moving on to the "more difficult problems" of transitional arrangements for an all-race election. Compromises were agreed which subsequently became a barrier to progress: for instance, the deeply entrenched protection of white-owned farms became a source of strife.

The interests of the mediator prevailed over those of the parties who would have to live with the consequences of these constitutional arrangements. In 1985, Robert Mugabe announced plans to amend the constitution to create a one-party state. Albert P. Blaustein, an American constitutional lawyer who acted as advisor to Muzorewa, wrote in a letter to the *New York Times* that Mugabe's intentions had been "readily predictable" at Lancaster House. Muzorewa had wanted a clause to guarantee the right to form political parties, but Blaustein claimed that "hidebound British lawyers objected – arguing that this was not in accord with their traditional independence constitutions".

More haste, less speed
Then as now, pressure to end the crisis carries the risk of miscalculation. An important lesson from history is that what appears to work in the short term, may fail over time. Constitutional reform must confront both the needs of the present and the demands of the future. Zimbabweans must learn from past mistakes and avoid the pitfalls which follow from the combination of crisis talks with constitution-making.

Zimbabwean politics has suffered a crisis of legitimacy at least since the elections of 2000. A constitutional process which includes a broad spectrum of political and civil society actors and restores public confidence in the political system is necessary to overcome the legitimacy deficit. For this reason, Zimbabwe's political parties should be encouraged to agree first on a democratic process to guide constitutional reform, and only then on the principles.

This process must incorporate mechanisms for Zimbabweans to express their views about the rules by which they consent to be governed. If constitutional reform is perceived as an attempt foist something on the people, the proposals of a political elite will be rejected – as occurred in 1999, when the government's attempt to adopt a new constitution was defeated in a referendum.

Debate about constitutional questions, inevitably, brings to the forefront divisive issues that political leaders may wish to avoid – as constitutional activists have discovered before in Zimbabwe, often at great personal cost. Addressing divisive issues is the purpose of all constitutional debate. The difficulty of this process is no justification for any attempt to curtail participation from the public.

In his role as regional mediator, South African president Thabo Mbeki should encourage Zimbabweans to take the path he advocated when his own country faced the challenge of crafting a new constitutional settlement. In his then role as the ANC's secretary for international affairs, Mbeki argued for the merits of an inclusive constitution-making process: "Free and popular participation is vital to the making of a constitution that has legitimacy in the eyes of the people," he argued in 1990. This legitimacy was "central to the exercise of democracy and to stability in a post-apartheid society".

Ultimately, the text of any constitution will be less important than the commitment of Zimbabweans to abide by its principles – in bad times as well as good. For this reason, the process matters as much as the document to the final outcome. Acrimony vented during negotiations makes it more, rather than less likely that a settlement will stick.

Emotions inevitably run high, as hopes and fears loom above the negotiating table. The sanguine can take heart from knowing that the painstaking work of reaching consensus is not about spectacle or individual triumph. Enduring constitutions rarely emerge in a burst of glory.

Gugulethu Moyo *is a Zimbabwean lawyer who works on southern African issues for the International Bar Association.*

A record of history

Judge Richard Goldstone *was a member of the first Constitutional Court in South Africa, and was previously Chief Prosecutor for the International Tribunals for Rwanda and the former Yugoslavia.* **Nicole Fritz** *asked him what Zimbabwe could learn from the political transitions of these countries.*

RG: All forms of justice, whether they are prosecutions, or truth and reconciliation commissions, or hybrid tribunals [such as Sierra Leone and East Timor] must provide a credible recording of what happened. That is essential to a successful transition.

The perpetrators of crimes against humanity always set up a system of denial. White South Africans believed even the most ridiculous explanations of why people died in detention. Recording the truth is really the only effective way to demolish such systems.

This is why the International Criminal Tribunal for the Former Yugoslavia is important. It really has stopped the denials in Croatia, Serbia and Bosnia-Herzegovina. All three nations regarded themselves as victims and the other sides as perpetrators. The testimony of hundreds of witnesses before the tribunal has forced them to accept that they were all perpetrators and all victims.

I think that's very important in building a peaceful future. The same is true in Rwanda. There were denials that there was a planned genocide. It was said it was a tribal explosion, but that is no longer even suggested – it would be ridiculous.

No one knows what the transition in Zimbabwe will look like. The South African government chose not to proceed with prosecutions. In Rwanda and Yugoslavia, on the other hand, there were prosecutions. In Zimbabwe, would transition need to involve prosecutions?

The type of criminality involved in those processes was completely different. You didn't have anything that approached genocide in South Africa, although certainly, apartheid constituted a crime against humanity. I think the South African amnesty process just made it – by the skin of its teeth. I'm sure today that it would be far more difficult to get international acceptance of amnesty for crimes of that magnitude.

But it should also depend on what the victims want. What is important about the amnesty provisions and the Truth and Reconciliation Commission is that they represent decisions taken by a democratically elected parliament, representing the victims. On that basis the international community accepted the process.

Of course, the International Criminal Court (ICC) wasn't around at the time of South Africa's Truth and Reconciliation Committee. The ICC represents the extent to which the international community has set itself against impunity and amnesties for the worst sorts of international crimes. This is a reality that would have to be taken into account in Zimbabwe.

The UN Security Council might refer the situation in Zimbabwe to the ICC in the same way that it did for Darfur. This has provoked criticism that the ICC is only being used to address atrocities committed in Africa.

The first prize is for a society in transition to manage that process itself. A Security Council mandate of investigation by the ICC would be a last resort. Were there a genuine intention to transform within the society, I don't think such a mandate would be helpful. But that would be for the people of Zimbabwe to decide.

Extracted from the *Mail and Guardian*, May 4th 2007, and edited for clarity.

The price of truth

Human rights lawyer **George Bizos** *defended Nelson Mandela, Govan Mbeki and Walter Sisulu at the Rivonia Treason Trial of 1963-4. In Zimbabwe, he has defended MDC leader Morgan Tsvangirai. His family came to South Africa from Greece as refugees from Nazi occupation, and he was closely involved in the formation of South Africa's Truth and Reconciliation Commission. He told* **Gugulethu Moyo** *that the rights of victims have to be weighed against other imperatives.*

GB: As apartheid was obviously about to come to an end, there was debate within South Africa, particularly in the African National Congress, as to what should happen to murderers, torturers, abductors. Then there were those responsible for forced removals and the implementation of apartheid. Three options were considered: Nuremberg-type trials, Chilean-style blanket amnesty, and collective amnesia along the lines of what had been tried in Argentina.

What was decided?
First, that we should devise a structure in order to grant amnesty. But certain principles would govern this amnesty. Secondly, amnesty would be on condition of full disclosure of all the facts. It would be granted for acts committed in order to achieve a political objective, not some outrageous motivation such as racial hatred or to settle old scores. Third, every act should have been proportional to the objective at the time.

An amnesty committee was set up, where applicants could be cross-examined. Amnesty could be granted or denied. It would be possible to prosecute applicants later, but the evidence given in the amnesty hearings could not be used against applicants in a criminal prosecution.

How did you arrive at this?
It was important to have an historical record, to show what happened. Many people in the apartheid regime said that human rights abuses were not sanctioned – there had been a few bad apples and the violations had not been widespread. These false denials would have gone on.

But the historical record shows that there were hit squads, torturers and abductors. The leadership should have known about them, and many in the lower ranks were protected by the leaders.

No one in their right senses could deny that this had happened – although we and our clients had been accused of being liars, propagandists for, and willing tools of, the enemies of South Africa.

Amnesty applicants in respect of the killing of the anti-apartheid activists, Steve Biko and Mathew Goniwe, confirmed the correctness of what we had said all along [about abuses committed by the security forces].

It was also a situation where something had to be offered to those willing to give up power. Otherwise, they would continue to cling to power. They threatened that unless they were covered by amnesties, they would fight on. We knew they had the means to control elections and to prevent any settlement.

In reaching this compromise, how were the interests of victims represented?
There was a political settlement. The Convention for a Democratic South Africa (CODESA) included 22 groups, mainly political parties. Bantustans [the nominally self-governing African homelands under apartheid] and leading liberation movements were part of it. But there was no coherent body to express the views of victims.

And the victims accepted this?
The settlement was challenged by the Azanian People's Organisation, the Biko family and some others. They challenged the validity of the law granting amnesty, which they said deprived them of their right to prosecution and the right to claim compensation from wrongdoers.

The judgment of the court in this case was very important. Judge Ismail Mahomed turned down their application. He said it was regrettable that the victims might not be able to pursue prosecutions, but their need for justice had to be weighed against the need for reconciliation and political transition and the need to uncover the truth.

Some victims complain now that compensation was inadequate and that those who did not get amnesty were not prosecuted. It is disappointing that the National Prosecuting Authority has not pursued those who should have been prosecuted.

> ## "All the different terms – retributive justice, restorative justice – indicate that justice is not absolute."

Did you address crimes committed by those in the liberation movements?
Once they agreed to conditional amnesty, the then government said that it must be an amnesty for all – not just for the government. Some of the acts committed by those in the liberation movement were dealt with.

The leadership of the ANC made a collective application to cover wrongs done by the ANC. That was rejected on the grounds that the perpetrators of abuses should not be granted amnesty as a group. There were individual acts carried out by individuals. Amnesty could not be given for nameless crimes. They never did re-apply. This is a serious concern. Justice was not done.

Is it enough just to tell the truth? Many of those who applied for amnesty did not do so out of remorse for what they had done.
It's a serious concern, but the answer is that justice is never perfect. All the different terms – retributive justice, restorative justice – all the adjectives used to describe justice seem to indicate that justice is not absolute.

One had to think, in a highly politicised situation, of what was morally justifiable. How many more innocent people would have been killed if we had not settled? You need to compromise.

But you did not know for certain whether the apartheid regime would cling to power.
Shortly before the compromise was agreed, at the end of 1993, representatives on both sides, particularly the security forces, threatened that the "men" would not accept it. This was taken to be a real threat.

Was there any pressure from abroad?
There was no foreign pressure. We reached a settlement because we believed it was the right thing to do.

The world has now changed and international law has changed considerably. These kinds of amnesties may not be an option now.

International law is to be welcomed, particularly because leaders who have committed serious crimes can be tried. One welcomes the establishment of the International Criminal Court, but regrets the lack of US support.

I believe that the international system does not necessarily exclude the domestic system. If, for instance, the people of the country are willing to hand over suspects like Milosevic and Charles Taylor, that means they have made their own decision. But in the case of Charles Taylor, would he have left Liberia if amnesty had not been granted? It's not clear-cut. It depends on the circumstances. If you look at what they have done in Northern Ireland, for instance, it's not an amnesty. It is a form of conditional release which is akin to what we did here.

You are still in contact with some of the victims. What do they say?

The victims wanted to know the truth about what happened. Most find it difficult to accept, for example, that the perpetrator is now the head of a private security company and drives a luxury car while the victims still live in poverty. This contrast shows the manifest injustice of it. But it may have to be that the good of the many prevails over the good of the individual. I'm sorry to say that, but that is the reality.

So, is South Africa a good model for political transformation? Should Zimbabwe – and other societies – follow this example?

South Africa is a good model. Yes, they must consider the solution we found.

Beating the watchdog

A free and courageous press has helped Zimbabwe, and can do so again. But fair elections are unlikely while the Access to Information and Protection of Privacy Act *remains in force. Veteran journalist* **Bill Saidi** *remembers the events which led to the bombing and banning of* The Daily News.

The parliamentary elections in 2000 were widely celebrated as a "watershed" for Zimbabwe – for good reason.

A new opposition party, just nine months old, had so galvanized the hitherto feeble voices of political dissent that ZANU-PF's grand design of a one-party state was thrown into confusion.

Four months earlier, in February 2000, ZANU-PF had been "thumped" in the constitutional referendum. The popular vote against the government was virtually the party's first electoral humiliation since independence.

The decline of a once-resilient economy had strengthened the opposition. On the electoral barometer, voters scanned the bread-and-butter issues and decided the MDC deserved a shot at the ultimate prize.

But another reason, perhaps not universally acknowledged, was the emergence of a stubbornly optimistic newspaper, *The Daily News*. The first issue was published in April 1999 and by February 2000, the paper was vying for readers with the state-run *The Herald*.

Challenging the government standard-bearer was no picnic. At *The Daily News* we told a story that *The Herald* would not tell – that 20 years of independence had not yielded the milk and honey for which nearly 30,000 people had died.

We hammered away to show how ordinary people had been marginalised, as corruption had eaten into our new nation. We worked to expose how the freedoms, for which people had died, were being slowly compromised by a ruling party.

As the 2000 parliamentary elections drew closer, *The Daily News* found itself attracting attention – from all sides. Some of this was undesirable, but most was the sort to make an editor walk tall among his peers.

By the time the election campaign was in full swing, *The Daily News* had come into its own. There is probably no unanimity to this day on the exact impact of *The Daily News* on the results of the 2000 election, in which the MDC won 57 of the 80 seats. But I have heard it said that if it had not been for *The Daily News* the results would have been different.

In 2000, *The Daily News* operated freely. But in 2001, a bomb blew up the printing press. Journalists, including editors, were harassed and detained. In April 2003, *The Daily News* and its Sunday sister, *The Daily News on Sunday*, were banned under the Access to Information and Protection of Privacy Act (AIPPA).

In the present atmosphere, the chances of a free and fair election in 2008 are slim. A vicious campaign is being waged against every dissenting voice. In response, the Zimbabwe Election Support Network has urged that: "The media, both private and state, should not be used to convey hate language and propaganda which hinders the holding of free and fair elections. There is also need for equal access to state/public media by all political parties."

How a government with its back to the wall is likely to respond to such recommendations is not difficult to predict. Unless regional heads of state insist on a personal commitment from Mugabe – preferably in writing – to unfettered and free reporting of all aspects of the electoral process, there will be no watershed poll in 2008.

Extracted from the *Mail & Guardian*, May 4th 2007, and edited for clarity.

In a rough neighbourhood

As SADC leaders map a recovery plan for Zimbabwe, **Geoff Hill** *argues that much can be learned from Rwanda and Somaliland.*[1]

It's amazing how fast a country can heal in the right hands. A return to the economic prosperity of the mid-'90s or even the early 1970s may take time, but Zimbabwe can come right.

There are countries, such as Rwanda and Somaliland, that serve as examples of what can be achieved in a new Zimbabwe.

In July 1994, Paul Kagame's forces overthrew the government in Kigali and stopped the genocide. They took command of a failed state littered with corpses. Today you'd hardly know it.

Tarred roads link all parts of the country, investment is growing faster than anywhere else in East Africa, and the currency is stable. As early as 2000, GDP had jumped by almost 50%. Rwanda is an easy place to do business and probably the most crime-free country in Africa. On the streets of Kigali are public telephones which work.

These are the decisive factors in the transformation wrought by Kagame:

- Depoliticising the police and public service.
- Bringing talent home from exile.
- Punishing corruption.
- Creating a relatively transparent government.
- Fostering growth in the private sector.
- Minimising demands for "local ownership".
- Lifting most restrictions on foreign exchange.
- Healing old wounds through legal trials for human rights abusers.

These are all challenges that face Zimbabwe.

Rwanda is almost a textbook case to follow – but not entirely. Kagame's biggest error has been to jail political opponents on spurious grounds. He has sought to limit freedom of the press by passing two acts of repressive legislation, provoking genuine resentment of his heavy-handed tactics.

There is a risk that these laws could undo Kagame's government. But in spite of these mistakes, Kagame has forged a template for rebuilding a nation from scratch.

An island of peace

Another example to Zimbabwe is less known, but even more impressive. The former British Somaliland achieved independence in 1960 and, a week later, joined with Italian Somaliland in the south to create Somalia.

The marriage was a disaster, with southerners in Mogadishu dominating the government. Under the one-party rule of President Siad Barre, festering resentments culminated in genocide in the north of the country. When a coup dislodged Barre in 1991, warlords took over the south and the country became partitioned.

Somaliland seized the chance to declare unilateral independence, on May 18th 1991. To this day, no other nation formally recognises the government in Hargeisa. But most countries accept their passports.

Somalilanders are rightly proud of their achievements. Whereas in Mogadishu, capital of Somalia, you can barely move without finding your path obstructed by an AK assault rifle, the only rifles I saw in Hargeisa were in the hands of soldiers, who were courteous, disciplined and well turned out.

As in Rwanda, the phones work and roads are reasonably good. Private capital is pouring in, mostly from Somalilanders living abroad. Somaliland has a GDP more than double that of Somalia, which is geographically four times as large.

I was struck by the example of sound governance and administration in Somaliland when I covered its general election of September 2005. If only Zimbabwe could have an election like that – with parties free to campaign, a total absence of intimidation, daily newspapers and even a TV station in private hands.

Still fragile

In case my description suggests paradise, I should caution that there are serpents in

Somaliland. The environment has been ravaged. Archived reports of commissioners from the 1920s describe a profuse variety of forests, savannahs and wildlife. Today the land is barren.

Almost the entire country has been denuded, as topsoil has washed into the Gulf of Aden. Aside from birds and insects, you'd be lucky to spot a rabbit among the dessicated plains. Ironically perhaps, Somaliland is luring displaced Zimbabweans to set up an agricultural sector.

Doctors are in chronically short supply. Literacy rates are improving, but still below 50%. In common with Rwanda and Zimbabwe, research suggests that much of the population suffers from post-traumatic stress.

Press freedoms are fragile. Earlier this year, Somaliland's leading independent daily newspaper, *Haatuf*, was closed down and four of its journalists jailed for between 24 and 29 months. *Haatuf* had published allegations of misuse of government property by the president and his family. The journalists were "pardoned" after an outcry by human rights groups, but the incident damaged the country's standing.

A new Zimbabwe can learn from, and improve on, these precedents. Exiles will need to return, investing their money in a rush of new capital, as happened in Rwanda and Somaliland. That can happen only when there is freedom – both political and civil – an end to corruption, a new police force and space for the media to operate without interference.

Can Zimbabwe be rebuilt in the short term? Rwanda and Somaliland are proof that others have achieved more against still greater odds.

Geoff Hill *is bureau chief, Africa for the* Washington Times *and author of* What Happens After Mugabe? *(Zebra-New Holland, 2005)*

A media worth the trouble

A raft of repressive legislation inhibits freedom of expression, restricting the role of the media in building democracy in Zimbabwe. **Tawana Kupe**, *dean of Humanities at the University of the Witwatersrand in Johannesburg, sets out a case for reform.*

Most countries in Africa have private and community-owned press and broadcasters which are editorially independent from government control.

Zimbabwe has not enjoyed freedom of expression, or of the media, for some years.

In the past 27 years, Zimbabweans have known only three years when privately owned daily newspapers were in circulation: the short-lived *Daily Gazette* and *The Daily News*.

Laws governing the media have been designed and operated to control the flow of information and open discussion. This has contributed directly to forestalling democratic change and reform.

After Mugabe, Zimbabweans need to make a clean break with this system of controlling the media. South Africa provides a useful example to follow.

Action needs to be taken to repeal laws, or sections of laws, which restrict the media. A new constitution must guarantee freedom of expression to ensure that the media is beyond the control of all-powerful interests, in particular the state.

The Access to Information and Protection of Privacy Act (AIPPA) is a misnomer. Instead of increasing access to information, it serves only to promote official secrecy. The law should be repealed and replaced with modern laws which require disclosure, promote transparency and can be applied as a weapon against corruption.

The statutory Media and Information Commission, which has power to license media houses and journalists, needs to be dissolved. The commission can be replaced by an independent and publicly funded agency with a mandate to promote media diversity. All newspapers that have been closed should be allowed to resume publication immediately. All foreign journalists who have been expelled must be allowed to return.

A new Broadcasting Act is required, which

removes control of broadcasting from the government and state ownership. As in South Africa and other democratic nations, there should be an independent authority to regulate the communications industry. Licences must be allocated by the independent regulator – and not the government – to enable the emergence of a diverse and pluralistic broadcasting system.

In this more open and competitive environment, an independent public broadcaster would compete for audiences with privately-owned stations. Community stations should be licensed to complement the public and commercial sectors.

The Public Order and Security Act and the Official Secrets Act, in their current form, are in conflict with the right to freedom of expression. These acts need to be repealed and replaced by laws which protect the freedom of the media to access and disseminate information in the public interest.

Sections of the Parliamentary Privileges and Immunities Act give parliament the power to sit as a court and imprison journalists. This is allowed in the case of journalists who reveal information obtained from parliamentary committees. These elements of the law impinge on freedom of expression and must be repealed.

In the case of serious grievance, a Press Ombudsman should be appointed to investigate complaints against newspapers; and for broadcasting, an independent Broadcasting Complaints Commission.

People who work in the media should form a voluntary, self-regulating Media Council to draw up professional codes of conduct. The council would monitor ethical violations and, when necessary, apply peer pressure and other sanctions to discipline errant colleagues. This kind of self-regulation does not inhibit freedom of expression, nor impinge on the independence of editorial and programming staff.

Zimbabweans will also have to develop, appreciate and defend a culture of freedom of expression as an integral part of a democratic culture. Freedom of expression and of the media belongs to all. The silencing of one is the silencing of all.

Extracted from www.mg.co.za/newzimbabwe, and edited for clarity.

After the plunder

Recovering the proceeds of economic crime to fund development will be the real test of efforts to curb corruption, write **Hennie van Vuuren** *and* **Charles Goredema**.

The great Nigerian writer, Chinua Achebe, would surely agree – to borrow from the title of his celebrated first novel – that in Zimbabwe things have indeed fallen apart. Gidean Gono, governor of the Reserve Bank, has described the country as a "fertile haven" for the endemic corruption which is "now part and parcel amongst the influential".

The example set by the political and business elite has trickled down to all levels of society. According to Transparency International's Zimbabwe National Integrity Study, corruption "is fast becoming a way of life. The vice has become so deep-rooted and institutionalised that some people now accept it as their sole means of survival due to a total collapse of systems that offer checks and balances."

Contrast this with Mugabe's strident claim of a "War against Corruption", echoing the American "War on Terror" in Iraq. In both cases, these are crusades against vices of these countries' own making. In spite of Zimbabwe's (toothless) Anti-Corruption Ministry and an Anti-Corruption Commission, the country has degenerated to a level at which both "petty" and "grand" corruption are an acceptable norm. Profit-seeking has become routine among the "wheeler dealer" elite, while the working poor extract bribes to supplement their salaries.

The occasional scandals reflect a deep-rooted decay in state institutions, as the government has systematically dismantled its National Integrity System, while at the same time restricting the space for free expression and legal investigation. The moral authority of a state which has, in effect, criminalised itself in order to regulate its affairs is called into question every day.

Striking similarities have begun to emerge between contemporary Zimbabwe and apartheid South Africa in the late 1980s and early 1990s. Although it was clear that bureaucrats and business leaders alike could see that change was inevitable, apartheid created vast opportunities to hide money. Among them were:

- A secretive Special Defence Account, worth up to US$40 billion, to buy political support for puppet regimes in the nominally self-governing *Bantustan* states.
- The oil and arms embargo, during which a proliferation of clandestine deals corroded basic standards of corporate governance.
- Involvement by the South African Defence Force in foreign wars in Namibia and Angola, with opportunities for ivory and drug smuggling.
- Proliferation of organised crime, including foreign exchange fraud and smuggling of precious metals and gems, with capital flight estimated at US$10 billion during the 1980s.

"Grand" corruption under apartheid has found a mirror image in Zimbabwe, where asset stripping and theft has again attracted criminal syndicates. The globally connected elite in Zimbabwe is operating in a similar way to its counterpart in apartheid South Africa. Among the most widespread corrupt practices are:

- Exports of gold and timber manipulated to conceal illegal transfers of capital abroad.
- Systematic looting of natural resources during Zimbabwe's military involvement in the Democratic Republic of Congo.
- Hoarding of stolen assets in order to buy off law enforcement agencies and investigations into the sources of new wealth.

In the light of these similarities between apartheid South Africa and Zimbabwe, a new democratic government in Harare would be wise to learn from the mistakes of its neighbour. South Africa has failed to deal effectively with corruption and economic crimes under apartheid. Economic crimes did not fall within the jurisiction of the Truth and Reconciliation Commission (TRC). The few investigations undertaken in the mid-1990s failed to secure prosecutions, amid reports that intelligence operatives were also corrupted.

Precedents for Zimbabwe

The success of the Jewish Claims Commission (JCC) in the 1990s established an important precedent for subsequent attempts to recover stolen assets. The JCC recovered funds looted half a century earlier by Nazi Germany from bank accounts in Switzerland. Following sustained pressure from civil society groups, including many African states, the United Nations in 2003 adopted a Convention Against

Corruption, in effect bringing the issue of asset recovery into the mainstream of policy.

The importance of the convention derives from the secretive nature of the international banking regime and the evidence of cooperation between corrupt elites and their host governments to conceal the proceeds of crime. By September 2007, 98 states had ratified the Convention. They have undertaken to return stolen wealth and to provide technical assistance to countries seeking to prosecute criminal elites.

The scale of funds involved is massive. The Commission for Africa Report of 2005 suggests that "stolen African assets, equivalent to more than half of the continents' external debt, are held in foreign bank accounts". While most African governments which have attempted to recover stolen assets have acted outside the framework of the UN Convention, their example is instructive:

Nigeria: Former president Olusegun Obasanjo "named and shamed" international banks which he claimed had received more than US$4 billion looted by the military dictatorship of Sani Abacha. To avert an expensive court battle with the Abacha family, Obasanjo's government agreed to forego US$100 million in exchange for the repayment of US$1 billion traced to the family's bank accounts.

Kenya: Incumbent president Mwai Kibaki was elected in 2002 on an anti-corruption ticket, but failed to recover any of the estimated US$3 billion in stolen funds held in foreign bank accounts. Attempts to investigate corrupt practices under Kibaki's predecessor, President Daniel arap Moi, have been hurt by evidence of renewed and systemic corruption under Kibaki. Kenya demonstrates the need for swift and decisive leadership before a new regime adopts the habits of the old.

Zambia: In May 2007 former president Frederick Chiluba was ordered by the High Court in London to re-pay US$46 million, after a civil claim by the government of Zambia, represented by the Zambian Attorney General. Chiluba was found to have unlawfully transferred state funds to a London bank account. However, the ruling must be registered in a Zambian court, and lawyers for Chiluba have contested the registration.

These cases demonstrate that laws alone are not enough to curb graft. Corruption has dogged Zimbabwe since the arrest of businessman Samson Paweni in 1982, on charges of defrauding the government over maize deliveries, and the "Willowgate" scandal in 1988, concerning the acquisition of motor vehicles for the elite. Most significant corruption cases were investigated and pursued through the courts, albeit reluctantly in some instances. At the level of both rhetoric and policy, Mugabe's government has taken steps to tackle corruption, organised crime and money laundering. A post-Mugabe administration will have to address the underlying causes of its predecessor's failure to make headway.

The first hundred days

The recovery of stolen assets provides an effective means of restoring public credibility in the justice system. Some analysts argue that a new government has little more than one hundred days to set the process in motion to trace stolen assets. Corrupt elements in government and business can be expected to deploy extortion and bribery in order to derail such efforts. If the cycle of impunity is to be broken, an incoming administration must adhere to the following principles:

Focus on private and public sectors: Although the state is often a source of corruption, private sector interests are often either complicit or victims of corruption; investigations should include both the relationship between state actors and corporate interests involved in government programmes of economic "empowerment" in Zimbabwe

Follow international guidelines: The UN Convention Against Corruption provides a mechnism for obtaining legal assistance and technical expertise to trace stolen assets; genuine assistance from the international community will signal to corrupt leaders that the immunity enjoyed in the past by Mobutu and others is at an end

Pursue regional cooperation: Neighbouring states such as Botswana, South Africa and Namibia should assist in tracing the proceeds of crime, in the form of property, bank accounts and other assets; Zimbabwe should become a test case for dealing with stolen assets in southern Africa.

Re-invent national integrity: By dislodging corrupt elites, a new government can credibly rehabilitate the National Integrity System to encourage accountable, responsive governance under a new constitution; separation of powers, freedoms of speech and association, and independent specialised anti-corruption agencies all contribute to depoliticising anti-corruption efforts under the auspices of a functioning democratic state

Avoid "peace at any cost": Corruption and economic crimes are often seen as negotiable during periods of transition, on the grounds that it is expedient to turn a blind eye to stolen funds during a delicate transfer of power; the knock-on effect is that the causes of corruption are likely to remain, as corrupt elites reinvent themselves under a new order

Formalise truth-telling: The examples of South Africa and Kenya confirm that the investigating of economic crimes is vulnerable to corruption and political interference; Zimbabwe should explore the option of an open judicial commission, and of including economic crimes as part of a restorative process – non-disclosure to the commission could result in prosecution.

The manner in which the new regime deals with economic crimes will determine whether it is able to break effectively with entrenched habits. Decisive action will encounter resistance from corrupt elites, but at great economic and institutional benefit to the country's poor. One only need reflect on the experience of modern African states in emulating some of the worst aspects of colonial rule, to realise that a clean break with the past is a priority.

Hennie van Vuuren *is head of the Corruption & Governance programme, and* **Charles Goredema** *is head of the Organised Crime and Money Laundering programme at the Institute for Security Studies in Cape Town, South Africa.*

No refuge for Mugabe

The International Bar Association, the world's largest international association of lawyers, has lobbied against amnesty for Mugabe. Chief executive **Mark Ellis** *told* **Gugulethu Moyo** *that leaders who commit crimes against humanity must be prosecuted under international law.*

Mark Ellis has vivid memories of the day he was invited for tea with the president of Zimbabwe. The chief executive of the International Bar Association (IBA), the world's largest international association of lawyers, remembers Robert Mugabe as a captivating host: "We were fêted as dignitaries, with drinks and food."

That was in 2001, when an IBA delegation raised concerns about the rule of law. In response, Mugabe made a number of commitments to his guests – a group which included Peter Goldsmith, now Britain's Attorney General, and South African advocate George Bizos.

Hardly had they stepped out of their meeting before the lawyers found themselves surrounded by television cameras from Zimbabwe's state media. "They asked very prejudicial questions and said we were biased, although the mission had not even given any report on its findings at that time," says Ellis. "Whatever hope we had that Mugabe was serious about resolving serious problems disappeared at that moment."

Ellis has campaigned vigorously for Mugabe and senior members of his government to be referred by the United Nations Security Council for prosecution at the International Criminal Court (ICC). His campaign has been dismissed by Mugabe's press secretary, George Charamba, who accused the IBA of "trying to tarnish the image of the president and the country". Mugabe's view is that "Zimbabwe is not part of the ICC and hence cannot be dragged into its counsels".

Ellis wants ICC chief prosecutor Luis Moreno-Ocampo to look closely at the record of government-sponsored torture, beatings and intimidation. Opponents counter that there is no consensus among the international community on how to prosecute international crimes. The US and several other countries are not party to the Rome Statute, while the first cases before the ICC are all from Africa.

Critics accuse Ellis of double standards. The IBA has not lobbied for the prosecution of US President George Bush or British Prime Minister Tony Blair, both accused of defying international law. Ellis denies the charge: "We have spoken out on the illegality of the war in Iraq, of the crimes committed in Guantanamo, on illegal renditions. So we are very consistent in upholding international standards."

The Rome Statute makes clear that the ICC will not intervene in situations where a country's domestic courts are able and willing to undertake the prosecutions. "Clearly in Zimbabwe the people are not able to do that. The ICC steps in where the national legal system is unwilling or not capable of holding individuals accountable," responds Ellis.

Other critics object that a campaign to prosecute Mugabe may not be in the best interests of a peaceful settlement in Zimbabwe. The negotiated end to apartheid in South Africa was helped by a commitment that leaders of the apartheid regime would not face prosecution. A similar process is underway in Northern Ireland.

The future for Mugabe is far from clear. The jurisdiction of the ICC in such cases is restricted to crimes referred for investigation by the UN Security Council. Both China and Russia have maintained close ties with Mugabe's regime and could use their veto to block moves to refer Mugabe to the ICC.

But Ellis remains determined. "No one thought the Security Council would muster up sufficient will to undertake the request [to refer Sudan for investigation]," he recalls. "I think Darfur gives us hope that the Security Council could find the will to act against Mugabe."

From Mark Ellis, *No refuge for Mugabe,* interview by Gugulethu Moyo, extracted from the *Mail and Guardian,* May 2007 and edited for clarity.

The road to free and fair elections

Constitutional Amendment 18, ratified by parliament in September 2007, allows parliament to nominate a successor to Mugabe. Elections are scheduled for March 2008, but **Welshman Ncube** *argues that a new constitution and an Independent Electoral Commission should come first.*

At the nub of Zimbabwe's crisis lies a succession of disputed elections beginning with the parliamentary elections in June 2000, through the presidential election of 2002 and the parliamentary elections of 2005. Unless and until Zimbabwe holds an election whose outcome will not be in dispute, it is very unlikely that we will see an end to the crisis. The most important question facing Zimbabwe today is what will it take to hold such an election.

The obstacles to holding free and fair elections are numerous, including an undemocratic constitution and a plethora of rigorously applied – and misapplied – repressive laws.

Free and fair elections are the foundation of democratic governance. Without free choice, elections become a charade, giving a veneer of legitimacy to a dictatorship. Because the government of Zimbabwe rules without the true consent of the people, it has resorted to coercion to defend its tenuous hold on power. This has created a vicious cycle of un-free and unfair elections resulting in disputed and illegitimate outcomes.

In its bid to muddy the waters, the government of Zimbabwe has deployed a whole array of propaganda tricks. Its appropriation of pan-Africanist and anti-imperialist ideals is a futile attempt to hide the true nature of the crisis.

A route to reform

The route to addressing all these issues begins with the making of a new national constitution. But there are also several key reforms which need to be implemented before the next elections, if they are to be free and fair. These include removing the obstacles to the enfranchisement of large sections of the population thought to be likely to vote for the opposition. Priority must be given to:

* Reform of electoral laws, particularly related to voter registration.
* Reform of repressive legislation to allow free political activity.

- A paradigm shift in political organisation away from the use of violence.
- An end to intimidation using food aid and traditional leaders.

The registration of eligible voters is frustrated by unreliable voters' rolls and the gerrymandering of constituency boundaries. The system is designed to exclude the youth and the urban poor, by giving more constituencies to provinces and rural areas believed to be ZANU-PF strongholds.

> *"With a truly independent electoral process, the manipulation of voters' rolls to disenfranchise millions of people will become easy to resolve."*

In the absence of a genuinely independent Electoral Commission, the entire electoral process lacks impartiality, transparency and fairness. There is a need for transparent auditing of key stages of the electoral process, starting with the printing and distribution of ballot papers.

In some cases, the protective provisions of existing electoral law are routinely flouted. Electoral officers, for example, have refused to announce and then display written results for each polling station. Other laws, notably the Public Order and Security Act, are abused to restrict the freedom of speech and assembly. Police have been granted powers to control, disallow and ban political meetings.

Media laws, in particular the controversial Access to Information and Protection of Privacy Act, curtail freedom of speech and fair reporting by the press. Independent newspapers have been shut down. The state monopoly of broadcasting has made Zimbabwe the only SADC country without even a single independent local radio or television station. Opposition voices have no access to large sections of the electorate, particularly in the rural areas where radio is the main means of communication.

Traditional leaders have also been manipulated by the state, becoming little more than local political commissars of the ruling party. Their role extends beyond partisan campaigning, as village chiefs and others in positions of traditional authority resort to an array of measures to coerce people into supporting ZANU-PF. Resettlement areas have been designated according to membership of, or support for, the ruling party, instead of taking account of local government and services. Support for the opposition has been punished by banishment and denial of access to land.

Under these circumstances, flawed elections have become a vehicle for consolidating dictatorship. They have brought violence, intimidation, misery and general suffering. Instead of welcoming the approach of elections as an occasion to celebrate their hard-won independence from an oppressive racist regime, Zimbabweans have come to view the prospect of elections with trepidation. They know that:

- Food aid has been manipulated as an instrument of political control, particularly in rural areas prone to shortages.
- Voter education has been restricted, with people denied knowledge of their political rights around election issues.
- The police, the army, the Central Intelligence Organisation and the civil service have been co-opted to serve the ends of the ruling party.
- The judiciary has been manipulated in order to remove any mechanism to resolve electoral disputes fairly and expeditiously.

A new constitution

The national crisis cannot be resolved until a legitimate and democratically elected government takes office. That in turn requires a free and fair election, which will become possible only if and when the rules and conditions of that election are accepted by both the ruling party and the opposition parties. In negotiations between these groups, the drafting of a new national constitution to broadly reflect a national consensus is top of the agenda.

A new constitution should entrench the right of the people to elect their government without hindrance. It must establish a truly independent electoral commission with exclusive responsibility over electoral matters including voter registration and control of all commission staff.

With a truly independent electoral process, controversy surrounding gerrymandering, manipulation of voters' rolls to disenfranchise millions of people, and systematic breaches of the electoral code will become easy to resolve. The electoral commission must be empowered to ensure that each and every voter who wishes to do so is able to exercise his or her right to vote without fear and undue bureaucratic hindrance.

The repressive provisions of the Public Order and Security Act (POSA), which have been used to ban political meetings and campaigns, must be repealed or amended. The overzealous application of the provisions of POSA by the police – to deny or limit the ability of the opposition to canvass support – has been so severe that it is impossible to imagine a free and fair election without an unconditional restoration of the right of free political activity.

The provisions of the Access to Information and Protection of Privacy Act (AIPPA) have been abused in order to persecute journalists. Freedom of expression has been severely curtailed by the closure of newspapers and unsuccessful prosecutions of journalists on questionable grounds. AIPPA must be repealed in order to restore freedom of the media, without which a free and fair election is impossible. State monopoly of the airwaves, under the Broadcasting Services Act, must be replaced by a new dispensation to allow independent radio and television stations.

In the best interests of the country, all those who love Zimbabwe should help ensure that the next elections are not held until there is national consensus on the electoral regulatory framework, including a new national constitution. Only then will the next elected government be accepted, by all fair-minded people, as legitimate. Only a legitimate government will attract sufficient domestic and international support to rescue Zimbabwe from its quagmire.

Welshman Ncube *is a lawyer and the secretary-general of the Mutambara faction of the Movement for Democratic Change.*

New rights for women

After a bold start at independence, Zimbabwe has paid lip service to international standards which protect women. The irony is that a government which claims to recognise human rights has behaved with impunity at home, writes **Fareda Banda**, *author of* Women, Law and Human Rights: An African Perspective.

It seems a lifetime ago that the government of Robert Mugabe demonstrated respect for Zimbabwean women by refusing a request from a visiting Iranian delegation that women should not be seated at the top tables at a state dinner.

The early years of independence brought the creation of a Ministry of Women's Affairs, headed by the current vice president, Joice Mujuru, and the introduction of a Legal Age of Majority Act which transformed the legal landscape for women. The Act proclaimed that, like men, at the age of 18 women became majors, able to enter into contracts by themselves.

Prior to this, the law defined African women as minors throughout their lives, passing from the guardianship of fathers to husbands. The Act was controversial. People argued that it encouraged daughters to disobey their parents and was a disavowal of "African culture". The government wobbled momentarily, but it held its nerve and refused to repeal the act.

More recently, in February 2007, the government enacted the Domestic Violence Act which seeks to provide both criminal sanctions and civil remedies for violence in the home or the community. Among the provisions is a statute to outlaw the traditional practice which forces a widow to marry the brother of her deceased husband.

While any law that seeks to advance the rights of women or to protect them from violence or other harmful practices is to be welcomed, one cannot escape the irony. A state that perpetrates violence within the public sphere, seemingly with impunity, has passed legislation seeking to outlaw violence within the private sphere.

Violence cannot be wrong in one context, but right in another. Clearly more must be done so that *all* people are considered equal before the law.

A flawed constitution

Zimbabwean women are failed by the constitution. It was amended in 1996 to outlaw gender discrimination, but this provision is weakened by a clause which states that in certain instances the law does not apply. These include issues of family law governed by custom.

Customary family law is the sphere most likely to affect the vast majority of Zimbabwean women. While there are many customs, and some families are generous in their interpretation of women's entitlements, justice for women should not be left to the mercy of family members.

Rather, the constitution should prohibit discrimination of any kind, without exceptions or exemptions being made for any legal system. Women's rights should not be made hostage to custom, culture or indeed religion.

Zimbabwe has ratified international human rights instruments, including the International Covenants on Civil and Political Rights (ICCPR), on Socio-Economic and Cultural Rights, and the Women's Convention. However, the government has not taken the important step, required by the Zimbabwean constitution, of passing a law to "bring the rights home". This would enable human rights norms to be applied in national courts.

Tellingly, the Zimbabwean government has also not ratified the optional protocols specified in either the ICCPR or the Women's Convention. These would allow citizens who felt that their rights had been violated, or who were not satisfied with the handling of their cases within the national legal system, to appeal to the United Nations bodies tasked with assessing complaints.

Serious consideration must be given to the ratification of the optional protocols and to the incorporation into the national system of those human rights instruments already recognised by the Zimbabwean parliament.

Fareda Banda, *New Rights for women*, extracted from www.mg.co.za/newzimbabwe and edited for clarity.

Varieties of justice

In the search for a better future there are useful precedents for confronting the past, writes **Priscilla Hayner**. *International law will be hard to defy.*

It is a mistake, in any country, to allow the past to deter or prevent change that would lead to a better future. But it would be no less mistaken to believe that events of today and yesterday will not fundamentally shape that future and the manner in which change takes place. The challenge and the aim of transitional justice is to encourage and strengthen a change – a transition – by finding reasonable and appropriate means to address the need for justice.

It is unclear what Zimbabwe's justice policies might become. A multitude of questions remain open, and will require a national debate and close scrutiny in order to find the right manner of addressing the past. The issues of accountability and responsibility for current and past human rights abuses, economic crimes and other trespasses are among the critical outstanding questions which will loom large in any transition.

Recent years have seen public institutions weakened and politically compromised. The judiciary, police and other security institutions need to be fundamentally reformed in order to build independent and fully functioning systems that can protect the rule of law. Luckily, Zimbabwe has a still recent history of independent and high quality institutions, and many talents to draw on.

Economic crimes will also have to be addressed, in the context of a quickly crumbling economy. The theft and destruction of property, severe economic hardship and deaths must hold a central place in any historical review, and in any national plan to come to terms honestly with the country's past.

In part because of the economic devastation, those now in power may well have two different worries in relation to any political change. The more obvious is the risk of being held to account. But, equally, many of those in positions of power are likely to depend on their current status for access to economic, health and other benefits. Some of these may be little more than basic, or sometimes lavish, perks. In other instances, the benefits may be life-saving. Political change that puts these advantages at risk will be strongly resisted.

Amnesty, from Charles Taylor to General Pinochet

Much concern or debate, though still not debated widely enough, is focused on whether President Robert Mugabe and others will, or should, receive an amnesty in order to facilitate a transition. Leaders of the opposition are not in agreement on this issue. Morgan Tsvangirai has said that he is willing to consider granting an amnesty in order to secure change. Arthur Mutambara, in contrast, has ruled out such an option and insists instead on a policy of "victim-based and restorative justice."

It is not clear how far any proposed amnesty might extend beyond the president, although it is known that many people have been complicit in abuses at both policy and operational levels. Meanwhile, fear of prosecution is understood to be a significant impediment to securing a peaceful resolution in negotiations with President Mugabe and those around him. Some may think that the best way to avoid prosecution is to remain in office for as long as possible, and it is apparently for this reason that some opposition leaders have favoured the offer of amnesty.

The international standards that have taken shape in recent years limit the possibility for such an amnesty. Legal obligations and prohibitions, which have been incorporated into international law through court decisions, treaty development and common state practice – referred to as "customary international law" – are now considered applicable to every state.

The United Nations, for example, has taken a firm line since 1999 in insisting on respect for principles which outlaw blanket impunity for certain serious crimes. These include genocide, war crimes and crimes against humanity. In effect, crimes of this order are now considered to be international crimes, deserving of international protection and attention.

In the context of Zimbabwe, it has been argued that crimes against humanity have taken place in recent years, and most particularly during the violent campaign of repression in Matabeleland in the 1980s. Crimes against humanity are defined as serious abuses committed in a widespread or systematic manner. The political reality, however, is that opposition leaders and the national parliament of Zimbabwe are independent actors and they may wish to grant immunity to persons, or groups of persons, regardless of the standards set out in international law.

If such an amnesty were unconditional, two questions would arise. The first is how the international community would respond to such an arrangement. In some contexts, donor states and others have strongly opposed amnesties that have been proposed in peace deals, even suggesting that future aid would be contingent on the removal of such clauses. The second question, which would be of concern to any recipient of an amnesty, is whether in fact such a blanket immunity arrangement will stick.

Restrictions set out in national law may already prohibit immunities in the case of serious crimes. Most national constitutions promise citizens access to the courts, and thus a blanket amnesty that prevented judicial access for past crimes could be found to violate the constitution. In any case, national laws only apply nationally. It is legally impossible to award an amnesty that extends outside the borders of a country. Recent developments in international law make such an amnesty even less palatable, and thus potentially would put recipients at risk.

The case of former Liberian president Charles Taylor has caught the attention of actors in Zimbabwe and elsewhere. Taylor was granted exile to Nigeria in 2003, only to be arrested two and a half years later and brought to trial. However, this should be recognized as a reaction in part to Taylor's own violation of the agreement under which the asylum was granted. One of the primary conditions of Nigeria's offer was that he refrain from involvement in Liberian or regional political affairs. It was widely believed that Taylor continued to meddle, from Nigeria, in the political affairs of the region through cell phone contact, and supported by his access to cash. Taylor continued to be seen as a potential destabilizing force until his arrest, and Liberians reported a sense of national relief when he was detained and turned over to the Special Court for Sierra Leone. His trial, concerning alleged crimes that took place in Sierra Leone, is scheduled to begin in early 2008.

Unlike Liberia, there is currently no international or hybrid court that has jurisdiction over crimes in Zimbabwe. It is highly unlikely that a new court will be created. President Mugabe is viewed as a hero by many African leaders and there would probably be little political will within the region to prosecute him in the same way. Rather than looking to Liberia, the more relevant precedent for Zimbabwe might be found in Latin America.

In Chile, former president, Augusto Pinochet, lived freely for years after departing from office under the terms of a self-awarded amnesty. After some time, and with the strengthened understanding of human rights principles, his amnesty was slowly stripped away. This first became evident with a legal challenge outside Chile. During a trip to London in 1998, Pinochet was detained and placed under house arrest at the request of a Spanish judge in Madrid.

Eventually, Pinochet was sent home rather than extradited to stand trial in Spain, due to concerns for his health. Back in Chile, he found his immunity weakened by a reinterpretation of the amnesty, as more robust courts became willing to act in human rights cases. This was not a case of a specialised international court pursuing a former head of state, but the result of a generalised strengthening of international human rights norms. The case of Pinochet demonstrates that restrictions on such norms may be challenged virtually anywhere, internationally or nationally.

Conditional and limited amnesties

Zimbabweans interested in receiving immunity could take the gamble. If national authorities decide to flout international standards on immunity, perpetrators of abuses can hope that a national amnesty would stand the test of time. Given the growing weight of international precedents, however, Zimbabwe might be smarter to stay within the law and accepted international parameters. These prohibit blanket and unconditional amnesty for international crimes, although it is not entirely clear what kind of judicial response and punishment are required. Again, Zimbabwe might look internationally, and especially to Latin America, for creative and appropriate responses that could be acceptable to all.

There are now many different types of amnesties. Stronger international standards and procedures have encouraged creative national responses which make every effort to stay within the bounds of international law. Many offer a process which differs from a strict legal regime of prosecutions.

A distinction should be made here between the potential conditionalities of amnesty versus the breadth of coverage: in other words, an amnesty might require certain actions on the part of the perpetrator, making it conditional – the amnesty could be revoked if such conditions are violated. Alternatively, whether conditional or not, an amnesty might explicitly exclude certain crimes, thus making it limited. Further, some amnesties are individualised, perhaps requiring an application process. Others, often referred to as "blanket" amnesties, cover a large group of people and are applied collectively.

In international law, the Geneva Conventions encourage amnesty for former combatants as long as serious international crimes are excluded. Amnesties that are conditional and individualised might be considered acceptable, depending on the nature and severity of the crimes covered.

The best known of these is the South African model, where perpetrators had to apply for amnesty for specific crimes, demonstrate that their crimes were politically-motivated, and fully disclose details of their crimes. Because the South African amnesty covered serious international crimes, experts disagree on whether this kind of amnesty regime would be seen to comply with international law in its current form.

More recently, more creative models of conditional arrangements have evolved whereby alternative or lesser sentences are offered which avoid amnesty *per se*. These go further than the South African model, requiring not only truth from the perpetrator, but also in some cases repayment of stolen assets – as in Colombia, or community service and apology – as in East Timor.

As I write, the most interesting experiment in conditional amnesty is taking place in Colombia. Persons responsible for serious crimes may receive considerably reduced sentences in exchange for disclosure of their crimes, cooperation with the peacemaking process and a contribution to victim reparations, among other requirements. While this has recently met legal challenges, it is an important case to watch carefully, as a testing ground for a scheme which provides incentives for perpetrators to cooperate with justice. Initially, at least, the Colombian arrangement has facilitated the demobilisation of an important government-aligned armed group.

A deep transition

Some legal and policy work on Zimbabwe in recent years has considered options for transitional justice. Many of the emerging recommendations have emphasized non-judicial approaches to justice, with a strong emphasis on rebuilding for the future. In particular, they have called for a truth inquiry, reparations for victims and fundamental reform of state institutions to prevent further abuse.

At a conference in Johannesburg in 2003, representatives of Zimbabwean civil society and international experts recommended a truth commission that would encourage disclosure from perpetrators. It also insisted that the inquiry extend to well before 1960.

Such a long historical view would be essential to take into account the abusive practices under white minority rule, and the legacy of this inequality which remains today. Such an inquiry would also need to consider the critical issue of land ownership.

A truth commission could also facilitate a deep transition in Zimbabwe. This approach to understanding and coming to terms with the past has become almost universally attractive, with over thirty such commissions operating to date in varied contexts around the world. Zimbabwe should be wary of too much influence from neighbouring South Africa, where the truth commission set up after apartheid was different in some important ways from those in other parts of the world.

> *"Because the South African amnesty covered serious international crimes, experts disagree on whether this kind of amnesty would be seen to comply with international law in its current form."*

Some aspects of the South African model resulted in significant frustrations on the part of victims and others. A robust process to respond to victims' needs, in parallel to a truth commission, would address some of these frustrations. The experiences in Peru, East Timor, Morocco, Sierra Leone and the truth commission recently set up in Liberia are instructive.

To construct an appropriate transitional justice policy, and the right institutions to carry it out, one must first identify the principal needs and public desires. A formal statement of truth, but with continued denial by state authorities or those directly involved, might be of little value to victims. In some contexts, acknowledgement and apology carries greater emotional weight for survivors than spelling out the specific details of events. In other cases, family members of those killed are most interested in recovering the remains, or at least knowing where the bones are buried. Attempts to cover up or deny serious and widespread abuses, such as in Matabeleland in the 1980s, may demand special attention.

In order to identify priorities and give shape to these programmes, Zimbabwe should undertake a process of broad public consultation. For practical purposes, this probably means that the specific mechanisms of a new transitional justice policy should not be determined until a political transition is underway. Only then will there be space for such an open conversation.

A further consideration may be the need to ensure stability immediately after a change in power. The consultation process, and the concomitant delay in determining the finer points of policy, could provide vital breathing space. Such a process should be seen by Zimbabweans as one of healing and rebuilding, while avoiding any suggestion of impunity. Impunity is no basis on which to build the rule of law.

Zimbabwe's future will indeed be shaped by its past. That fact is true everywhere and would be hard to escape. Getting to the future – in particular a positive future, involving change and rebuilding – means grappling with this past, as difficult as that is, and confronting the depth of damage that has been done.

Priscilla Hayner *is co-founder of the International Centre for Transitional Justice and director of its programme on peace and justice in Geneva.*

AN INVITATION TO THE GOVERNMENT OF ZIMBABWE

Africa Research Institute

President Robert G. Mugabe
Government of Zimbabwe
Munhumutapa Building
Harare

Via Fax + 263 4 703 858 and + 263 4 703 820

September 21st 2007

Your Excellency, President Mugabe,

The Day After Mugabe
Prospects for Change in Zimbabwe

I write to invite a contribution from you, or on behalf of your government, to a book to be published by the Africa Research Institute. At a time of acute hardship for most Zimbabweans, we hope to collect for the first time fresh and forward-looking thinking on realistic prospects for recovery.

I am sincere in assuring you that the ambition of this book is honest. It was not conceived as a partisan project. The book begins with your own Eve of Independence speech on April 17, 1980 and includes more recent commentaries from President Thabo Mbeki of South Africa, Zimbabwe Reserve Bank governor Gideon Gono, and Sir Sonny Ramphal on his experience as secretary-general of the Commonwealth during the Lancaster House talks in London in 1979. Contributors span a wide range of perspectives – both local and from Beijing, London, Lusaka, and Pretoria.

We would very much appreciate your analysis of Zimbabwe's prospects, an assessment of the likely possibilities for presidential succession, and your hopes for the future. We undertake to publish any contribution in good faith. As you may be aware, I have briefed your representatives at the Embassy of Zimbabwe in London on the content of this book.

The Africa Research Institute is a new and non-partisan think-tank based in Westminster. Our mission is to draw attention to ideas that are working well in Africa, and to encourage fresh thinking in adversity. We will ensure copies are sent to all Commonwealth heads of state, plus relevant policy-makers, diplomats, development agencies and donors. The contributors to this book are of diverse loyalties and experience, united by the hope that it will contribute to a wider understanding of Zimbabwe and development of more effective policies for the future.

Yours sincerely,

Mark Ashurst
Director

43 Old Queen Street London SW1H 9JA UK | t. +44 (0) 20 7222 4006 | f. +44 (0) 20 7222 8959 | e. info@africaresearchinstitute.org
www.africaresearchinstitute.org
Registered charity 1118470

President Robert G. Mugabe
Government of Zimbabwe
Munhumutapa Building
Harare

Via Fax + 263 4 703 858 and + 263 4 703 820

September 21st 2007

Your Excellency, President Mugabe,

The Day After Mugabe
Prospects for Change in Zimbabwe

I write to invite a contribution from you, or on behalf of your government, to a book to be published by the Africa Research Institute. At a time of acute hardship for most Zimbabweans, we hope to collect for the first time fresh and forward-looking thinking on realistic prospects for recovery.

I am sincere in assuring you that the ambition of this book is honest. It was not conceived as a partisan project. The book begins with your own Eve of Independence speech on April 17, 1980 and includes more recent commentaries from President Thabo Mbeki of South Africa, Zimbabwe Reserve Bank governor Gideon Gono, and Sir Sonny Ramphal on his experience as secretary-general of the Commonwealth during the Lancaster House talks in London in 1979. Contributors span a wide range of perspectives – both local and from Beijing, London, Lusaka, and Pretoria.

We would very much appreciate your analysis of Zimbabwe's prospects, an assessment of the likely possibilities for presidential succession, and your hopes for the future. We undertake to publish any contribution in good faith. As you may be aware, I have briefed your representatives at the Embassy of Zimbabwe in London on the content of this book.

The Africa Research Institute is a new and non-partisan think-tank based in Westminster. Our mission is to draw attention to ideas that are working well in Africa, and to encourage fresh thinking in adversity. We will ensure copies are sent to all Commonwealth heads of state, plus relevant policy-makers, diplomats, development agencies and donors. The contributors to this book are of diverse loyalties and experience, united by the hope that it will contribute to a wider understanding of Zimbabwe and development of more effective policies for the future.

Yours sincerely

Mark Ashurst
Director
Africa Research Institute
43 Old Queen Street
London
SW1H 9JA

NOTES AND REFERENCES

INTRODUCTION
1 Wole Soyinka, speech to the Royal Commonwealth Society, London, March 26ᵗʰ 2007.

1. THE HOME FRONT

Calling in the generals
1 Jonathan Moyo and Xolela Mangcu, *The Weekender,* August 4th 2007; Trevor Ncube at Witwatersrand University, August 1st 2007; Ibbo Mandaza, preface to *A Lifetime of Struggle,* Edgar Tekere, Harare: Sapes Books.
2 Janowitz, M., 1960, *The Professional Soldier: A Social and Political Portrait.* Glencoe: Free Press.

2. ECONOMY AND LAND

How many farms is enough?
1 Sachikonye, L.M., 2003. 'From growth with equity to Fast Track reform: Zimbabwe's land question.' *Review of African Political Economy,* 96:227-240.
2 Ibid.
3 British High Commission, 2007. *Zimbabwe and Land.*
4 Moyo, S., 2007. The Land Question in Southern Africa: A Comparative Review. In R. Hall et al (eds). *The Land Question in South Africa.* Cape Town: HSRC Press.
5 Sachikonye, op.cit.
6 British High Commission, *op.cit.*
7 Moyo, op.cit.
8 Presidential Land Review Committee, 2003. Report of the Presidential Land Review Committee under the chairmanship of Dr Charles M.B. Utete, Vol 1 and 2: *Main report to The President of The Republic of Zimbabwe, August 2003.*
9 Chigumira, E., 2006. *An appraisal of the impact of the Fast Track Land Reform Programme on land use practices, livelihoods and the natural environment at three study areas in Kadoma District, Zimbabwe.* Unpublished M.Sc. Thesis, Rhodes University, Grahamstown, South Africa.
10 World Food Programme, 2007. WFP Appeals for 118 Million Dollars Food Aid for Zimbabwe. http://www.medindia.com/news/WFP-Appeals-for-118-Million-Dollars-Food-Aid-for-Zimbabwe-24436-1.html Accessed August 2nd 2007.

"We are printing money to build roads and dams"
1 Extracted from the August/September 2007 edition of *New African* magazine and edited for clarity.

Zimbabwe's golden leaf
1 Goodman, J., 1993. *Tobacco in history: The Cultures of Dependence.* London: Routledge.
2 Maravanyika, E. The economics of tobacco in Zimbabwe. In *The Economics of Tobacco Control in South Africa.* Cape Town: School of Economics, University of Cape Town, June 1998.
3 Ibid.
4 'Cotton replaces tobacco as top forex earner', *IRIN (Integrated Regional Information Network)* February 23rd 2004.
5 'UN development boss 'ruined Zimbabwe farm'', Thornycroft, P., *Sunday Telegraph,* March 12th 2007
6 British American Tobacco website http://www.bat.com/

7   Keyser, J.C., 2002. *The Costs and Profitability of Tobacco Compared to other Crops in Zimbabwe*, HNP Discussion Paper, Economics of Tobacco Control, Paper No. 1.
8   Zimbabwe: ICT at a Glance, World Bank.
9   Interview with Emma Priestley, Aoiffe O'Brien, September 10th 2007.
10 Interview with the Foreign and Commonwealth Office, Mark Ashurst, August 8th 2007.

3. AN AFRICAN DILEMMA

Taking Africa's name in vain

1   *The Herald*, Harare, July 7th 2007
2   'SADC Needs Inviolable Electoral Standards', Mutasah T., *Sunday Independent*, Johannesburg, September 25th 2005
3   Elie Wiesel, Nobel Peace Prize acceptance speech, Oslo, December 10th 1986

Rough justice

1   This is a revised version of a report first broadcast in March 2002 on the BBC's *From Our Own Correspondent.*

5. TRANSITION

In a rough neighbourhood

1   Extracted from the *Mail & Guardian*, April 20th 2007, and edited for clarity.